# The Qur'an

*A Biography*

# The Qur'an

## *A Biography*

BRUCE LAWRENCE

Grove Press
New York

*Printed in the United States of America*

Library of Congress Cataloging-in-Publication Data
Lawrence, Bruce B.
    The Qur'an : a biography / Bruce Lawrence.
        p. cm. — (books that changed the world)
    Originally published: London : Atlantic Books, 2006.
    Includes bibliographical references and index.
    ISBN-10: 0-8021-4344-x
    ISBN-13: 978-0-8021-4344-0
    1. Koran—Evidences, authority, etc.    2. Koran—Commentaries—
History and criticism.

B130.74.L39      2007
297.1'22—dc22            2006048555

Design by Richard Marston

Grove Press
an imprint of Grove/Atlantic, Inc.
841 Broadway
New York, NY 10003

Distributed by Publishers Group West
www.groveatlantic.com

08  09  10    10 9 8 7 6 5 4 3 2 1

For Dr Ibrahim Abu Nab, who lived the truth of 'seeking God's purpose every day'. (Qur'an, Chapter 55:29)

# CONTENTS

## EARLY COMMENTARIES

## LATER INTERPRETATIONS

## ASIAN ECHOES

## GLOBAL ACCENTS

# ACKNOWLEDGEMENTS

My debts are too many to permit more than brief acknowledgement here. My first and enduring debt is to Ibrahim Abu Nab of Amman. A gifted translator, journalist and film-maker, Ibrahim opened his heart as well as his home to me when I visited him back in the 1980s. We spent long evening hours reading, discussing and translating the Noble Qur'an. I have benefited from his insight into A Book of Signs (the Qur'an is at once the Noble Qur'an and A Book of Signs. See below pp. 8 & 15) and his reverence for its divine origins. I honour his memory by dedicating this book to him.

In several chapters I have used some of the privately circulated translations of Shawkat Toorawa. I am indebted to him for permission both to cite his lyrical renditions and to modify them slightly in this biography of A Book of Signs. Equally am I beholden to five of my former students, Rick Colby, Jamillah Karim, Scott Kugle, Rob Rozehnal and Omid Safi, for their extraordinary insight into the shaping and reshaping of this text. To my colleague, Ebrahim Moosa, who read the whole of the manuscript with the heart of a believer and the eye of a critic, I give special thanks. My life's partner, Miriam

Cooke, did so much that no words of mine are adequate. I invoke Rumi. Quoting the Prophet's dictum, Mawlana once observed that 'women totally dominate men of intellect and possessors of hearts'. May this book be its beneficiary!

# A NOTE ON TRANSLATIONS

Notes on translation are as necessary with respect to the Qur'an as they are futile. No single translation in English satisfies. The closest is Thomas Cleary, *The Qur'an: A New Translation* (Starlatch Press, 2004), often cited, or paraphrased, in the chapters above. It completes his earlier, condensed effort, *The Essential Koran* (HarperSanFrancisco, 1994), which some may still prefer, if only because it, unlike the 2004 rendition, offers an introduction and partial commentary. The most satisfying English translations with commentary and/or textual apparatus are A. J. Arberry, *The Koran Interpreted* (Macmillan, 1955) and M. A. S. Abdel Haleem, *The Qur'an: A New Translation* (Oxford University Press, 2004). For those who want both an English translation and the Arabic original with which to compare it, Ahmed Ali has provided *Al-Qur'an: A Contemporary Translation* (Princeton University Press, 1988).

The Qur'an exceeds the efforts of the most skilled and dedicated translators. It must be heard to be appreciated in its Arabic cadences, its inexpressible rhythms, its calibrated scales. The most available partial recitations can be found in the audio CD that accompanies Michael Sells' original, evocative study, *Approaching the Qur'an: the Early Revelations* (White Cloud Press, 1999).

For an insider's introduction to the elements of traditional and progressive interpretation of the Qur'an, consult Farid Esack, *The Qur'an: A Short Introduction* (Oneworld Publications, 2002), and for the delights and dilemmas of teaching the Qur'an in the modern European or American university, see Jane D. McAuliffe, 'Disparity and Context: Teaching Quranic Studies in North America' in Brannon M. Wheeler (ed.), *Teaching Islam* (Oxford University Press, 2003), pp. 94–107.

Jane D. McAuliffe is also the General Editor for what will be the major reference work in English on the Qur'an for at least the next fifty years: *Encyclopaedia of the Qur'an* (E. J. Brill, 2001–2005). Its five volumes total slightly less than 2,700 pages, and include extensive cross-referencing as well as some illustrations in volume 2.

# A NOTE ON ROMANIZATION

There are several styles for rendering Arabic words into English, and throughout I have followed the most popular usage, so that the Prophet Muhammad is spelt differently from Imam W. D. Mohammed, though both are the same word in Arabic, and most feminine names end with –*ah*, though they can also end with just –*a*. For those who know Arabic these choices are arbitrary, while for others they are minor details worth noting but without lingering on their importance.

# INTRODUCTION

The Qur'an discloses key elements about itself. Specific verses clarify the meaning of its name, the affirmation of Islam as true religion, and the priority of peace.

1. The name Qur'an means recitation:

> We have sent it down with truth,
> and with truth has it come down,
> and We have not sent you (Muhammad)
> except as a herald and a warner.
>
> And We have divided the Recitation (Qur'an)
> that you may recite it to humankind at intervals,
> and We have sent it down by (successive) revelations.
> (17:105–6)*

* This, and all subsequent references, are to the Chapters and verses of the Qur'an.

2. Islam is true religion:

> The true religion with God is Islam. (3:19)

> If anyone seeks a religion other than Islam,
> it will not be accepted from him. (3:85)

> Today I have perfected your religion for you,
> and I have completed my blessing upon you,
> and I have approved Islam for your religion. (5:5)

> Whomever God desires to guide,
> He expands his breast to Islam. (6:125)

And finally, in a rhetorical question:

> Will not he whose breast God has expanded to Islam,
> walk upright in a light from his Lord? (39:24)

Since the word 'Islam' means complete devotion or surrender
(to God), the rhetorical question of the last verse lays down
the fundamental duty incumbent on each Muslim: to 'walk
upright in a light from his Lord'.

3. Peace is the priority:

> God summons humankind to the abode of peace (*dar
> as-salam*), both in this life and in the next. (10:25)

So closely is the concept of peace (*salam*) related to surrender (*islam*) that the two become interchangeable, from the first revelation till the final Day of Judgement.

It is angelic intermediaries who mark the first revelation of the Qur'an, and they mark it with greetings of peace. During the Night of Power, when the Qur'an is said to have been revealed in its entirety to the Prophet Muhammad,

> Angels and the spirit alight,
> On every errand by God made right
> Peace reigns until dawn's early light. (97:4–5)

Similarly, when the faithful enter Paradise, they will be greeted by angels uttering the phrase, '*As-salamu 'alaykum*,' ('Peace be upon you') (7:46; 13:23–4; 16:32). Everywhere in the Muslim world, as also among Muslims living outside the majority Muslim regions of Africa and Asia, one uses the greeting '*As-salamu 'alaykum*', to which the response is '*Wa-'alaykum as-salam*' ('And upon you, too, be peace').

But the return greeting can also be lengthened. This habit derives from, even as it reinforces, the Qur'anic command:

> And when you are greeted with a greeting,
> greet with one fairer than it, or return it. (4:86)

The 'fairer than it' is often spoken if people have not seen each other for a long time. To make the response 'fairer than it [the original greeting]', a Muslim may outdo the greeter with a cadenza of good wishes: '*wa-'alaykum as-salam wa-rahmatullahi wa-barakatuhu*' ('And on you be peace, and (also) God's mercy and (also) His blessing').

In every instance, peace here in this world relates to peace in the next world. Chapter 36, Ya Sin, attests the clear and ever-present link. When the Day of Judgement arrives, it will come as

> But a single cry, when lo!
> They are all brought before Us. (36:53)

And then from the Sovereign of the Day of Judgement ('*malik yawm ad-din*', 1:3) will come:

> Peace ! A word from a Merciful Lord! (36:58)

Hence the everyday greeting of peace that unites believer to believer in this world anticipates the peace pronounced by God on the Final Day, the Day of Judgement.

*

Beyond disclosing its name, affirming Islam and stressing peace, the Qur'an has other key characteristics that deserve mention.

Revelations are sorted out into Chapters and verses, and the causes of each revelation provide context for its content. The number of revelations exceeds 200. They came to the

Prophet Muhammad via a divine mediary (the Archangel Gabriel) between 610–632 CE. They are now arranged in 114 Surahs or Chapters. All but one (Chapter 9) begins by invoking God's Name, then qualifies the Name as at once Compassion and Compassionate: 'In the Name of God, Full of Compassion, Ever Compassionate'. Different people close to the Prophet Muhammad heard these revelations as he uttered them. They remembered the words and repeated them orally. A few wrote them down. In all they total at least 6,219 verses.

The contents of Surahs (Chapters) and ayat (verses) are informed by the causes of revelation, that is, by events and circumstances that marked the Prophet's life and the early Muslim community. They have two major emphases. The first and shortest revelations came in the Meccan period (610–622). Invoking heaven and hell in anticipation of the Day of Judgement, they call polytheists to worship God as One. They also call Jews and Christians to recognize Muhammad as the seal of prophecy fulfilling for the Arabs and humankind the mission set forth for earlier prophets. Abraham and Moses are the principal prophets from the Torah, John the Baptist and Jesus the principal prophets from the Gospel. The later revelations, because they came after the *hijrah*, or flight from Mecca to Medina, are known as Chapters from the Medinan period (622–632). They share images and persons, themes and categories from the early, Meccan period but they are at once longer and more directed to social, political and military issues.

Naming of the Chapters became crucial for their recall and

recitation. Sometimes the name came from a word or theme mentioned in the Chapter. Certain Chapters have several names because they are important for multiple reasons. 'Surat al-Fatihah' is the first and the most often recited. Though it is called 'The Opening', it is also known as the 'Mother of the Book' or the 'Seven Oft-Repeated Verses'. Chapter 17 is known as 'The Children of Israel' but also as 'The Night Journey', since its initial verse alludes to the most unusual journey of the Prophet Muhammad: he flew on a winged steed from Mecca to Jerusalem, from Jerusalem to the Highest Heaven, then back to Jerusalem and Mecca, all in a single night. (The journey may have been a dream sequence or an out-of-body experience but was nonetheless real; see Chapter 1 below.) Chapter 112, one of the shortest Chapters, is so pivotal that it has been labelled by its dense but complementary themes 'The Unity' or 'The Sincerity' or 'The Nature of Lordship'. Still other Chapters are known by mysterious letters that occur in the first verse, like 'Ta Ha' (20), 'Ya Sin' (36) and 'Qaf' (50).

Through a complex process, the recitations that had been revealed in verses and chapters became over time a book. After the death of the Prophet Muhammad, 'Ali, his close relative and supporter, worked with others to compile them into a written text. Then twenty years later, during the rule of 'Uthman, the third Caliph or Successor to Muhammad (after Abu Bakr and 'Umar but before 'Ali), all extant versions were arranged into one 'standard' version. This version persists substantially unchanged to the present day.

The earliest copies of the Qur'an were written in a script called Kufic Arabic, which had no vowel signs. It was for a further forty years, during the rule of the Umayyad Caliph 'Abd al-Malik (685–705), that the first written version of the Qur'an with diacritics was produced. Seven different ways of reciting the Qur'an were also fixed, but that occurred still later, *c.* 934 CE. The same seven forms of Qur'an recitation have remained a canonical standard ever since.

*

The emphasis on recitation is not accidental. It is central to understanding the formation and the force of the Qur'an. The Qur'an is a book unlike any other: it is an oral book that sounds better spoken than read silently, but it is an oral book that is also a scripture. More evocative in recitation than in writing, the Qur'an is only fully the Qur'an when it is recited. To hear the Qur'an recited is for Muslims unlike anything else. It is to experience the power of divine revelation as a shattering voice from the Unseen. It moves, it glides, it soars, it sings. It is in this world yet not of it.

The Qur'an was first enunciated by the Archangel Gabriel to the Prophet Muhammad in early seventh-century Arabia. What Muhammad heard then must be heard again and again, from now until the end of time. Hearing the Qur'an recited is the compass of spiritual insight and moral guidance for Muslims. It is the message in its pure form, a form at once starkly pure and vivid.

The Qur'an is a multilayered Arabic text. Even those who hear it understand it in numerous, sometimes divergent ways, and those who cannot hear it in Arabic grasp no more than a fraction of its intended message.

The limits of human experience affect the way we approach the text. The Qur'an as written in Arabic is less than the revelation given to Muhammad; it is a second-order revelation. The Qur'an written, then translated from Arabic to English, becomes a third-order revelation. Distance from the source handicaps us, yet we can still learn about Islam by engaging with the Qur'an, even as a written text, translated from Arabic to English.

The Qur'an rendered into English projects an echo, at times a loud echo, of the vibrant spiritual core of Islam. Whether one hears or reads it, in Arabic or some other language, it is A Book of Signs because each of its many verses, like delicate filigree, is more than words: the Arabic word for the smallest unit of Qur'anic text means 'verse', but 'verse' also means 'sign' or 'miracle'. As tangible signs, Qur'anic verses are expressive of an inexhaustible truth. They signify meaning layered within meaning, light upon light, miracle after miracle.

To make the Qur'an accessible to a broad and varied readership, I have arranged this book as a series of vignettes which can be read consecutively or selectively. To offer a thematic thread, the fifteen vignettes are divided into five sections of three, entitled 'Arab Core', 'Early Commentaries', 'Later Interpretations', 'Asian Echoes' and 'Global Accents'.

Each vignette has a distinct geo-historical context and is marked by a specific date in the span of Muslim and world history. The exception is the last vignette. Just as the Qur'an speaks across epochs, so the use of Qur'anic passages and invocation of God's names have no temporal or spatial limit. The last vignette could also be the first: its attention to the sick is unbounded by either time or space, even though AIDS, one of its topics, is a virulent, contemporary disease.

Still, there is a storyline, and it cannot be ignored. It is framed in Arabia with an Arab core. In 610 a Meccan merchant, while meditating in a mountain-top cave, heard a voice summoning him from beyond to be a messenger. He was given messages, which were disclosures, or revelations, from on high. What became the Qur'an transformed the way Muhammad thought about himself, his society and the world. These revelations prompted him to challenge kin and clans, to motivate others to follow him, to form a new community and to make that community the centre of a new movement. There followed skirmishes and warfare, alliances and treachery which changed his life but did not alter his purpose. He was confirmed as the Prophet, the final Prophet, of God. His name was Muhammad ibn Abdallah, the religion revealed to him was Islam, the centre of Islam was Mecca (and then, after the *hijrah* or flight, Medina as well as Mecca).

During Muhammad's lifetime, but even more after his death in 632, Muslim armies fanned out in all directions from Mecca. They confronted long-established empires adjacent to Arabia. To the east they attacked Hindu coastal cities in

Gujarat and Sind. To the north they swept through the Persian Sassanian Empire. They swiftly toppled it, claiming Iraq and Iran as part of a new Islamic polity by the mid-650s. To the west, Muslim armies quickly conquered Egypt but then moved less rapidly across North Africa, fighting both Berbers and Byzantines until they reached the Atlantic Ocean in the 680s. It was a military conquest that occurred faster, and with more consequence, than the spread of the Roman Empire seven hundred years earlier. It made Arab armies, and navies, the major controlling force of both the Mediterranean and the Indian Ocean. It also expanded the audience for the Qur'an beyond what could have been imagined in the lifetime of the Prophet.

This book traces specific ways in which the Qur'an was experienced within the growing Muslim community. The Prophet's young wife 'A'ishah became a major figure in its transmission, as did a descendant of 'Ali, the Shi'ite Imam Ja'far as-Sadiq. Monuments as well as persons transmitted the text and projected the authority of the Qur'an, none more so than the Dome of the Rock. Built in Jerusalem within a century of the Prophet's death and on the Temple Mount, hallowed for both Jews and Christians, the Dome of the Rock memorialized the Night Journey of Muhammad, the journey that took him from Mecca to Jerusalem to Heaven to Jerusalem then back to Mecca. The Dome of the Rock etched the Night Journey with words of the Qur'an. They are words that have preserved until today the earliest written verses of the Qur'an.

However, not all Christians or Jews accepted the Qur'an as true or Muhammad as God's Prophet. Among the doubters was Robert of Ketton, a Christian monk, who first translated the Qur'an into Latin. His role as a hostile but engaged student of A Book of Signs deserves mention along with the parallel role of major Muslim interpreters who elaborated Qur'anic themes in new and imaginative directions. Two of them were Persian: the ninth-century scholar at-Tabari and the thirteenth-century poet Jalal ad-din Rumi. Another was an Andalusian Arab, the twelfth-century mystic, Muhyi ad-din Ibn 'Arabi.

The commentary of at-Tabari, together with the interpretive approaches of Rumi and Ibn 'Arabi, had an impact on the large and varied Muslim community of India. From the seventh century India had been linked to the global Muslim community. Known as Hindustan, the Asian subcontinent or South Asia today encompasses the current nation-state of India as well as India's biggest neighbours, Pakistan, Bangladesh and Afghanistan. Hindustan has been a major platform for the growth of Muslim communities, and remains today a vast arena for the expression of Islamic loyalty.

South Asian Muslims approach the Qur'an from a cultural domain shaped by language and outlook that are Islamic but not Arab. Open to outside influences, they filter what they receive through their own distinctive aesthetic imagination. Of fifteen vignettes, three come from South Asia. The first focuses on a royal woman who was memorialized in her burial space: the Taj Mahal. The Taj Mahal is a seventeenth-century tomb that is at once simple and complex. Its marble surfaces project a unity that forever changes, from morning to evening light. It is fronted by a water pavilion, surrounded by mosques and geometrical gardens, and banked against the Jumna River. The Qur'anic inscriptions on the marble surfaces of the Taj Mahal tell the story of its intent. The Taj Mahal proclaims a view of the next world etched by the Qur'an and echoing Ibn 'Arabi in its visionary breadth.

India has also produced several notable male interpreters of the Qur'an, two of whom are included here. One was the nineteenth-century rationalist Sir Sayyid Ahmad Khan. Sir Sayyid welcomed the pragmatic values of the British, especially in governance and education. To the extent that modern science embodied the metaphysical values of modern Europe, however, he challenged its superiority and countered with an alternative modernity based on the rigorous retrieval of Qur'anic values. In this sense, he was the precursor to Muhammad Iqbal, the most famous Indian, then Pakistani, interpreter of Islam in the twentieth century. A poet-philosopher, Muhammad Iqbal was not a Qur'an interpreter, either by intention or by reputation. He engaged European philosophy and modern science as twins, each reinforcing the authority of the other, yet he saw both as inseparable from the larger message of Islam over time that was presented in the Qur'an. Iqbal was a citizen of the modern world, intent on reconciling reason with revelation. Resolutely Muslim, he projected in verse a perception of Qur'anic truth that was pervasive and superior to all other truths, including modern philosophy.

All the vignettes in this book illustrate a recurrent, essential point: while the Qur'an itself is a unitary, coherent source of knowledge, there is not a single Qur'anic message. The Qur'an – like all sacred literature – requires study. The act of studying its form, content and transmission over time is called interpretation. For the Qur'an, as for the Torah or the Bible, interpretation requires a form of human labour inseparable from the conscious or unconscious decisions of the labourer. Each interpreter must choose. Each must follow a principle of interpretation. No matter who the interpreter, no matter the time or place from which she or he looks at the Qur'an, certain themes, issues and accents will be selected and emphasized over others. The major difference is between narrow and broad selection of Qur'anic texts, or more precisely, between taking certain verses and passages out of context rather than viewing them in their full context when making claims about a normative Islamic world-view.

But selection is not the same as invocation. Nearly all Muslims invoke the Qur'an – as ritual authority, as everyday guide, as artistic motif, or even as 'magic'. Some memorize the Noble Book from youth, honouring the tradition that prizes its orality or spoken quality as the bedrock of truth. Even for those who do not memorize all of its 6,000-plus verses, its words acquire an everyday rhythm. They can be put around the neck in an amulet; they can sit on taxi drivers' dashboards, in rear windows or on bumper stickers; they can be carved into stone or scratched into metal or used to grace a letterhead. Written on an alphabet or prayer board, they can also be washed off and drunk for curative purposes. Even a Muslim who doesn't know Arabic or has never learned the Arabic of the Qur'an, respects the book, can recognize when others use it, and may draw on its syllables and sounds in everyday life. Consider the sick woman mentioned below. She uses the Qur'an as a magical force, invoking its words whether through whispering them, smelling them or drinking them. Such are the popular means of making the Qur'an one's own touchstone for healing and for hope. Even though many have contested this as a blasphemous use of the Qur'an, such use, as well as the controversy surrounding its use, will continue for the rest of this century and beyond.

No one can exhaust the Qur'an, as the book itself attests:

> Say, even if the ocean were ink
>> For (writing) the words of my Lord,
>> The ocean would be exhausted
>> Before the words of my Lord were exhausted,
>> Even if We were to add another ocean to it. (18:109)

The fifteen vignettes only hint at the surfeit of meanings that make the Qur'an unique. What they are intended to do for the reader, whether Arab or non-Arab, Muslim or non-Muslim, is to engage both the text and the context of the Qur'an. Contexts are crucial. Although the Qur'an as a whole is authoritative, its content must be applied to particular contexts. Which aspect of the Qur'an applies and where? When does it apply and for whom? These are questions that probe coherence and selectivity at two levels: first, why are some but not all passages of the Qur'an of special value at different times and places?; and secondly, how do changes in context impart special value to particular verses or Chapters?

The crucial criterion for interpreting the Qur'an is history. In a historical context the Qur'an becomes A Book of Signs, multilayered in its meanings, continuously reinterpreted by successive generations and diverse audiences. Detached from history the Qur'an becomes *the* Book of Signs, singular in its meaning, applicable across time and place, unchanging, univocal.

Is the Qur'an plurivocal or univocal? Devout Muslims are divided. Those who assert that it is univocal occupy one perspective within the interpretive community of Qur'an users. They have been called fundamentalists but they are better understood as absolutists, since they see the Qur'an, and by extension Islam, as primordial. It has a heavenly prototype, 'umm al-kitab', literally, the Meta-Book, which is the full record of God's Word. The Qur'an as a perfect reflection of the heavenly prototype is not like other words or books. It is above time and beyond history; it remains untouched by human temperament or by temporal change. Absolutists can exist in different eras. Osama bin Laden had his precursors in the seventh-century Khawarij, early Muslims who rejected any human mediation of God's Word. In common with the Khawarij, bin Laden decries the departure of Muslims from a single, 'true' interpretation of Qur'anic revelation and social action. When he invokes the Qur'an, he projects it as a single, unchanging message.

For the militant Muslim minority, the necessary sequel to professing the faith is defending the faith. Instead of daily prayer, alms-giving, fasting and pilgrimage – all deemed to be essential practices, or pillars of piety, for most Muslims – the very next step required of all believers, in the view of militants, is to wage *jihad*. They justify *jihad* not as moral struggle but as all-out war. Citing certain passages from the Qur'an, they uphold them as singular in meaning and valid for all time. The duty of every believer is to sacrifice himself or herself in defence of the faith through armed combat.

Yet neither bin Laden nor other absolutists speak for all Muslims. Militant Muslims remain a fractious minority who stress the confrontational aspect of monotheistic faith. Other Muslims demur. Notable amongst them is the voice of Imam W. D. Mohammed (see chapter 13). An African-American Muslim leader, he has provided guidance to millions of his co-religionists who had previously defined Islam by race as much as by creed. Since the 1960s he has led them into mainstream Islam and also into mainstream America. Imam Mohammed contests that the Qur'an provides a staging ground for apocalyptic warfare. For him the Qur'an does require *jihad*, but it is not *jihad* as all-out war. It is *jihad* as an eternal battle between good and evil. The highest temporal pursuit for Muslims, in his view, is to be pragmatic citizens of a twenty-first-century global community. Deeply grounded in a Qur'anic world-view, Imam Mohammed remains open to engagement with non-Muslims. He seeks allies in a larger war against poverty, racism and environmental degradation. He values a world at peace where the true *jihad* is for justice, not armed conflict motivated by hatred or displayed as terror. Though absent from mainstream media, his voice is as important as Osama bin Laden's. Like the sick woman who derives her hope from Qur'anic traces, Imam Mohammed provides a vital, contemporary invocation of A Book of Signs in the twenty-first century.

# Arab Core

## CHAPTER 1

# The Prophet Muhammad: Merchant and Messenger

619 CE

Muhammad was a merchant with a message. The message was not his own nor did he seek it. The message sought him, filled him and transformed him, making his life a journey that none, including he, could have imagined.

His humble circumstances did not suggest the lofty destiny that he claimed. Muhammad was born in Mecca into the clan of Banu Hashim about 570. It was a clan of declining importance, eclipsed by the rival Banu Umayya. He was also disinherited by virtue of his birth: a posthumous child, he had not reached maturity when his grandfather also died, and so he was excluded by Arab custom from any paternal inheritance. Because most of his closest relatives were merchants, Muhammad accompanied his uncle Abu Talib, his closest surviving male relative, on trading journeys to Syria. He learned the ways of a caravan leader well enough to be employed by a woman merchant, who was also a widow, named Khadijah.

Khadijah asked Muhammad to marry her. He consented when he was about twenty-five and she about forty years of age. After marriage he continued to trade with her capital and in partnership with one of her relatives. He became acutely aware of the disjunctures in Meccan society. He pondered his own good fortune to have survived the perils of the orphanage thanks to a protective uncle and then a supportive wife. At regular intervals he would leave his wife to go with his young cousin 'Ali to the caves on Mount Hira near Mecca. There he fasted and meditated.

While grateful for the gifts of family and wealth, he still lacked something. It was that lack which drove him to the mountain retreat, to find a space within himself and apart from others, to ponder the mystery of human success and the lessons of human failure.

Like many of his tribe, he had acknowledged the power of the rock that marked his hometown of Mecca. The Ka'bah (a cube-shaped sanctuary for idols) contained that rock, which was also linked to an early seeker of truth, a prophet in his time, named Abraham. It was to this place that Abraham sent his concubine Hagar and, with divine guidance, made provision for a branch of his family:

> Our Lord, I have settled
> a part of my progeny
> in a barren valley
> near Your Holy House,
> our Lord,
> that they may be constant in prayer,
> making the hearts of some folk incline to them

> and providing them with fruit,
> that they may give thanks. (14:37)

But the Ka'bah had become a crowded Holy House. It had become a place that Abraham shared with others, with idols that represented local gods and tribal deities. These idols were said to possess a power that rivalled the God of Abraham. Some folk who came to Mecca cast doubt on the power of the idols, saying that after Abraham came other seekers of truth, other prophets, each proclaiming a god not found in idols. Some opponents of the idols were the Jews, whose prophet was Moses. Other opponents were the Christians, whose prophet was Jesus, though some of them went further, claiming that Jesus was more than a prophet.

Muhammad also met some Arab opponents of idol worship. They claimed that there was an ancient Arab prophet, Salih by name, and that he too followed the way of Moses and Jesus, looking for the source of all life and all created forms, beyond idols of any shape or any place. It was Salih who said to his people what was later revealed to Muhammad:

> O my people, serve God,
> you have no god but Him.
> He brought you forth from the earth
> and made you dwell in it.
> So ask forgiveness of Him,
> then turn to Him.
> Surely My Lord is Near and Responsive. (11:61)

Muhammad meditated on these matters when he used to sit in the cave of Hira during the holy month of Ramadan. Ramadan was the time each year when blood feuds were suspended, and when Meccans who had wealth and free time could retreat to the outskirts of their town, to the hills that enclosed them, and to the caves that offered shelter and repose.

Muhammad had been following this practice for over a decade. Then one night in Ramadan in 610 CE, when he was about forty years old, he felt a strange stirring inside him. He loved the night-time in this special month; it drew him deep into himself and allowed him to resist those impulses that pulled him back to the world, to concerns with family or with business or with travel. He was alert to repel those impulses: they clouded his vision, they denied him peace of mind, but above all, they blocked his search for the truth. But this was a different stirring. It was deep, it was arresting. It overpowered him, and then it produced words, words that were not his. 'Recite!' And he was shown a piece of silk with words embroidered on it. 'What shall I recite?' he asked. 'Recite!' came the command, and again the brocade was thrust before him. He stammered: 'But what shall I recite?' Muhammad could speak but he could not read. All those who accompanied him on caravan trips, whether to Egypt or Syria, to Yemen or Abyssinia, knew that he could read symbols but not words. It was they who handled the few documents of exchange that required reading or signing. When Muhammad had to sign, he would ask others to read aloud what was written, then he would sign by pressing the palm of his hand to the paper. Why then did this voice ask him to recite?

Even as he was thinking these thoughts, for the third time, the voice commanded him: 'Recite!' 'But what, what shall I recite?' No sooner had he spoken than the words appeared:

> Recite in the name of your Lord who created,
> Created man from blood coagulated!
> Recite for your Lord is Most Generous,
> Who taught by the pen,
> Taught what they did not know unto men! (96:1–5)

These words became part of him. He recited them without reading them. But why did they invoke the Lord as *his* Lord? And why did they rhyme? 'Created' rhymed with 'coagulated' in the first two lines, and then 'pen' with 'men' in the fourth and fifth lines. Since Muhammad could not read the words, he was puzzled, dismayed. Had it been his secret impulses that had produced these verses? Had he become a man possessed, an ecstatic poet such as his clansmen distrusted, even despised? Was his pursuit of the truth forfeited by a single moment of self-deceit?

Scarcely had he absorbed the experience when his whole body began to tremble. Then the voice spoke again. It addressed him by name: 'O Muhammad!' 'O Muhammad,' it continued, 'you cannot protect yourself from the Evil One. Only the One who hears all and knows all can protect you. Invoke God but before you mention God by His loftiest name, say "I seek refuge from Satan, the Accursed, in the name of the One who hears all and knows all." Before you repeat the words I have just given you from Your Lord, say: "In the name of God, Full of Compassion, Ever Compassionate!"' and the silence descended.

He waited for more counsel. He needed advice. What was he to do? Where should he go? How was he to make sense of this? But nothing more came. He got up and bolted down the mountain, running towards Mecca, towards home, towards Khadijah, his beloved wife. Halfway down the voice returned. Now it was a booming voice with a face, a man's face. The face appeared to come from beyond the horizon. The celestial form announced: 'O Muhammad, you are the apostle of God, and I am Gabriel.' He tried to look away, but wherever he looked, there was the face; there was the man, staring at him.

He could not move. He was frozen on that spot. For a long time he stood there, until finally his wife Khadijah sent scouts to look for him. They found him and brought him home. As soon as they left he collapsed into his wife's lap. He told her what had happened on this strangest of days atop Mount Hira. 'O son of my uncle,' she exclaimed, addressing him with the same name that she had when she had proposed marriage to him some fifteen years earlier, 'O son of my uncle, be at ease and rejoice. In the name of the One who enfolds the soul of Khadijah, I can dare to hope that you have been chosen to be the prophet for this people.'

A prophet for his people?! How could a mere merchant

attuned to meditative silence become a messenger who must proclaim the message, often against his own deep wishes and even more, against the preferences and practices of his people? Every prophet, after all, is also a rebel. Muhammad had never seen himself in this role. Nothing in his life had prepared him for the period of trial that now beset him. His wife and also his young cousin came to view him in a different light. He was still their close companion, but now they saw him as one separate, apart, more respected than loved, though always cared for, his words and wishes heeded. Yet others were less kind, even rude, often taunting him for his 'poetic' outbursts, his 'pretended' inspiration.

But the greatest obstacle for Muhammad was silence; long, seemingly endless periods of silence. If he were worthy of this high calling, why did the voice that came to him not come more often and more insistently? He had to endure long periods when there was no inner voice. Whenever he did hear the voice, he would repeat what he heard so that others could remember the exact words. Above all, he depended on his beloved and trusting wife, Khadijah. She became the first Muslim, a woman to honour all women and to make them companion believers with men. And after her came his young cousin, that boy 'Ali, who was so quick and constant in his affection for Muhammad.

By 619 he had had many communications from beyond. Though the fear of being a possessed seer or ecstatic poet had passed, he lived every hour in the shadow of that protective phrase known as the *basmalah*: In the Name of God, Full of

Compassion, Ever Compassionate. Each time that the voice spoke, he repeated these words to make sure that it was indeed the Lord of Life who was speaking to him, not the accursed one, Satan, slinking into his mind, whispering in the garb of God.

Yet even the *basmalah* could not overcome the hostility of some in his town. Many of his clansmen and fellow Arabs had come to accept his new status as an apostle among them. Yet the more popular he became, the louder were his detractors. One day in 619 he had suffered more abuse than even he could bear. That night, in despair he had called out to the voice, and to the Lord of Life. He had begged for some sign that he might endure and, if God willed, that he might prevail against his adversaries. What happened next was both vivid and unspeakable. In the words of an anonymous poet:

> *He came to me, wrapped in the cloak of night,*
> *Approaching with steps of caution and fright.*
> *Then what happened, happened; to say more fails.*
> *Imagine the best; ask not for details.*

It was a night that reminded Muhammad of that first night, the Ramadan night when Gabriel had come to him as a voice, as a face, as a presence that could not be denied. Later it had been revealed to him that that first night was to be the Great Sign containing even as it unfolded all that followed. It was the Night of Power, heralded in the Noble Qur'an:

We have revealed it in the Night of Power.
How can you know what is the Night of Power?

Better is the Night of Power
Than a thousand months, hour for hour.
In it angels and the spirit alight,
On every errand by God made right
Peace pervades till dawn's early light. (97)

The second revelation, the Night Journey, followed that Night of Power. Both nights were shrouded in mystery yet they contained and defined the life of Muhammad more vividly than any daytime event. It seemed as though a mere instant separated one from the other, or perhaps time itself had been transformed by the Unseen. While the Night of Power had brought the majesty of heaven to earth to an un-suspecting messenger, the Night Journey propelled him to another place and finally to a celestial destination. The Night Journey took Muhammad from Mecca to Jerusalem and then to the highest throne of heaven. The familiar voice of Gabriel announced what was to happen. It beckoned Muhammad to ascend to the Source of all Truth and Life, the Touchstone of Peace and Justice:

By the star when it sets,
Your companion neither worries nor frets
Nor does he ever speak with regrets.
It is only revelation that he begets,

It is One mighty in power who projects,

And propels him upward to what perfects,

Far beyond the horizon where the sun sets,

Nearer and nearer to the source he trajects,

So close that a mere bowline between them intersects.

    (53:1–9)

Muhammad was first transported on a winged steed to the rock where Abraham nearly sacrificed his son Ishmael in the ancient city of Jerusalem. Jerusalem was the abode of prophets, from Abraham to David to Jesus. Now it hosted the Arab prophet, the Prophet Muhammad. Dazzled, he was transported by Gabriel himself from that rock up to heaven. At the first level of heaven many angels and the Prophet Adam greeted him. At the second level it was other prophets, Jesus and John the Baptist, who hailed him. At the third level he met still other prophets, Joseph and Solomon, and at the fourth level he encountered Moses along with his sister, Miriam. Onward and upward he continued to progress. 'It is One mighty in power who projects.' Arriving at the fifth level, he met the prophets Ishmael and Isaac, then the prophets Elijah and Noah at the sixth, until finally at the seventh level he was dazzled by yet another chorus of angels. In their midst was the greatest of prophets, the Prophet Abraham. Abraham greeted Muhammad warmly before sending him on to the Lote Tree of the Limit (53:14).

Here 'near the Garden of Return, when the tree was covered in nameless splendour' (53:16), Gabriel spoke on behalf of the Glorious and Exalted One. He offered Muhammad and his community Divine Beneficence if they would but pray fifty times per day. Muhammad nodded and retreated. But as he began to return to earth Moses reminded him that fifty prayers were too many for his Arab followers. Muhammad returned. He requested a reduced protocol of piety. Gabriel became his arbiter. Twenty-five prayers? Ten prayers? Finally Muhammad was granted a divine reprieve: from that day till the Day of Resurrection, incumbent on him and all his followers was the daily recital of five prayers, a mere five times of prayerful remembrance to punctuate each day with thoughts and desires directed solely to the Lofty One.

And then the vision was over. Muhammad descended by the same celestial route that he had ascended. He returned to the Temple Mount in Jerusalem from where he had begun his ascent, and then on the same winged steed back to Mecca. The next morning Muhammad awoke still stunned by the Night Journey yet comforted, his confidence restored.

He needed confidence to face the many trials that were to beset him in Mecca. One trial was perhaps the most tiresome and occurred soon after the Night Journey. It was as though the Compassionate One had wanted to test whether he would become prideful in his own role as messenger. Even though he was the one chosen to repeat God's message to all Arabs, and to all humankind, he was still a mortal, a mere man like other men.

Muhammad was reminded of those gods of the Ka'bah

that his tribe had worshipped before the Lord of the Ka'bah had called them to look beyond such idols, and to reject their intercessory power.

> Have you then considered Lat and Uzza,
> And another, the third, Manat?
> Are the males for you and the females for Him? (53:19–21)

Were these rhetorical questions, or was this an invitation to reconsider the intercessory power of the three idols? Muhammad may have hesitated but the Divine answer came in the next sweep of revelation:

> This is indeed an unfair division!
> They are only names that you yourself have named,
> You and your father; God has not granted them a position.
> They follow but fancy and what their lower selves
> requisition.
> It is only from their Lord that they find guidance and
> decision.
>
> Does man get whatever he hankers for?
> No, all that has gone before and all that comes after
> Belongs only to the Lord of Life, to God! (53:22–5)

Since that first revelation on Mount Hira some seven years before, Muhammad had never felt so close to the line of distinction between what came to him from above and from below. Once there were revealed to him words that sounded like a talisman, an amulet to ease his troubled soul. They were words that he repeated often when he felt the need for divine protection from other words, other whisperings that were not from above but from below:

> In the name of God, Full of Compassion, Ever
> Compassionate
>
> Repeat: I seek protection with the Lord of Creation
> the King of Creation
> the God of Creation
> From the malicious incantations
> Of the Accursed, whispering insinuations
> In the hearts of jinn and humankind both,
> fabrications. (114)

What were these staccato-like phrases if not a divine incantation? Muhammad felt their power, and their comfort, especially when he was confronted with disbelievers, and especially with rival messengers. One such was Musaylima, who claimed the power to counter ambivalent spirits (jinn) and, above all, the least ambivalent and most lethal of spirits, Satan. Musaylima identified himself as an apostle of the One beyond all comparison, even sometimes calling him the One Full of Compassion (*Rahman*). And what was the 'proof' of his prophecy? Rhymed prose utterances similar to those Gabriel revealed to Muhammad.

Yet, neither Musaylima nor any other so-called apostle could produce a book like this Qur'an in Arabic. Muhammad's people, like Jonah's people, were warned, not just about the Day of Judgement but also about false prophets. It is in the Chapter revealed as the sign of Jonah that the Lofty One declares to Muhammad:

> And this Qur'an is not something
> that could be manufactured without God;
> rather, it is a confirmation of what came before
> and a clear explanation of the (eternal) Book –
> there is no doubt in it – from the Lord of all creation.
>
> Do they say that He has forged it?
> Say: let them bring a chapter like it,
> and call on anyone whom you can besides God,
> if you are truthful. (10:37–8)

Because the Lord of all Creation had revealed His Word to Muhammad, he felt sustained against both doubters and imitators. He had been given not just the five daily prayers, but also the creed, the alms for the poor, the fast of Ramadan and the pilgrimage to the Lord of Ka'bah, all through the Qur'an. The Qur'an was an invitation. It was also an outpouring of Divine Favour into the human domain, into the human heart. The Qur'an announces God's Mercy in the opening chapter. Its seven verses offer the gist, the fine gold dust, of all revelations. It channels Divine Abundance through seven portals of hope, each verse conferring Divine solace on those who remember and those who recite these words. Collectively, the seven verses of the opening chapter became the gateway to spiritual health, for all believers, be they Jews, Christians or Muslims:

In the Name of God, Full of Compassion, Ever
Compassionate

Praise to the Lord of all Creation
Full of Compassion, Ever Compassionate
Master of the Day of Determination.

You alone do we worship
And from You alone do we seek alleviation.

Guide us to the path of True Direction,
The path of those whom You favour,
Not of those who cause You anger,
Nor of those who took to the path of deviation. (1)

Vouchsafed by these words, by the intermittent announcements of Gabriel, by the salutary Signs from the Unseen, Muhammad had begun his journey as a messenger of God. He had become a vehicle for the Divine Word. At the same time, for his enemies he remained a rebel against his own people. He had reviled their rites at the Ka'bah; he had defiled the gods of their ancestors. By 619 his journey had just begun. The orphan merchant had become an inspired messenger. Yet even he could not have imagined where this journey would take him during the next decade, for the rest of his life, and beyond.

## CHAPTER 2

# The Prophet Muhammad: Organizer and Strategist

632 CE

Since the time of his first revelations Muhammad had been buoyed up with hope by his wife Khadijah. Khadijah became the first believer, and as a devout Muslim she comforted him from his first revelation until her dying breath. Muhammad was also protected by his uncle Abu Talib, who did not become a Muslim yet honoured his kinsman. However, another uncle, Abu Lahab, together with his wife, confronted and tormented Muhammad. The raw opposition of this uncle and aunt dismayed him, but then there came a further counsel from the Unseen, exhorting Muhammad that to be a prophet he had to withstand such terrible men and women, and that God would be his final protector.

> In the Name of God, Full of Compassion, Ever Compassionate
>
> > Abu Lahab and his power
> > Both will expire.

> He will not be saved by wealth
> Or the profits he may acquire.
>
> He will be plunged
> Into lahab, a burning fire!
>
> And his wife –
> That kindling-carrier –
> Her neck shackled by palm fibre! (111)

Hellfire awaited those who disobeyed God and heckled His Prophet. Yet, despite the Divine promise, death awaited not only Muhammad's foes, like Abu Lahab and his wife, but also those who were closest to Muhammad, his most intimate and trusted supporters. In 619 he lost Khadijah, his wife and confidante, and also Abu Talib, his uncle and father by trust, and his protector against hostile clansmen and other Meccan detractors.

Muhammad became vulnerable to loneliness and to persecution. Threatened by Meccan opponents, he sought help in other oasis towns, amongst other tribes. He began to think the unthinkable, that he could not survive except at a distance from his native town and his tribesmen.

Muhammad's main channel of communication to the outside was through the annual fairs held on the outskirts of Mecca. At these events, recognized as intervals of truce, even his bitterest opponents could not assail him. More than commerce took place. News about events in Arabia and beyond circulated at these fairs. At one such fair in 620 Muhammad met representatives from a tribe to the north. They met again the following year. They responded to the Qur'an, they accepted Islam, some had even begun to pray publicly on Friday. These were people from Yathrib, later known as the city of the Prophet or Madinat al-nabi, and today simply as Medina.

In Mecca the opposition to him and to his message continued to grow month by month. Muhammad had sent some of his family to Abyssinia earlier, including his precious daughter Ruqayya and her husband 'Uthman. They remained there, protected by a generous and wise Christian king, but Muhammad needed another refuge within Arabia. The town of Medina seemed like his best hope. He could go there but not without risking conflict with his neighbours and clansmen from Mecca. To make this move, he needed help from the Unseen and this help came to him in a further Sign from God:

> In the Name of God, Full of Compassion, Ever
> Compassionate
>
> > Permission to fight is given to those on whom war is
> > made,
> > because they are oppressed.
> > And surely God is able to provide them victory
> > (over their oppressors).
> >
> > Those who are driven from their homes without a
> > just cause

> except that they say: Our Lord is God.
> And if God did not repel some people by others,
> Cloisters, and churches and synagogues, and
>     mosques
> – in all of which God's name is remembered –
> All would have been pulled down.
> And surely God will help him who helps Him.
> Surely God is Strong and Mighty. (22:39–40)

These precious verses provided the solace he sought, and the command he needed, in order to flee with his closest supporters to Medina. There, with God's help, he could, and he did, begin a new life as the mediator of other groups' conflicts. At the same time he continued to be the vessel of the Divine Word, the reciter of those blessed phrases that came from beyond, from the Archangel Gabriel. The year of his flight (*hijrah*) was 622. The flight marked the beginning of a new moment, and also a new calendar: 622 became the first year for that community who accepted Muhammad – those who prayed with him, fought for his cause, and those who, like him, waited for guidance from beyond through Gabriel.

Yet Muhammad did not cease to be a reciter once he became a community advocate. He organized the five ritual daily prayers, and at the same time oversaw construction for what became the first mosque. But now he also faced choices as a military strategist. He had to defend his community against those who either betrayed or assaulted him.

His enemies included some of the neighbouring tribes, but all of them were connected in some way to Mecca, either to his close relatives or to tribesmen. It was not always clear whether they opposed the radical message of Divine Oneness which Muhammad proclaimed or were allied with clan members who worried about their loss of influence if the new Muslim community succeeded. Some of them were spiritual men, like Suhayl ibn 'Amr, leader of the 'Amir clan of the Quraysh. Others, like Abu Sufyan ibn Harb, leader of the 'Abdu Shams clan of the Quraysh, were less spiritual but no less upright. They were both formidable fighters and honourable leaders. Then there were younger Meccan nobility, like Khalid ibn al-Walid of the Makhzum clan and 'Amr ibn al-'As of the Sahm clan. Neither accepted Islam yet they remained high-minded.

However, there were still others who both opposed his message and assaulted his person, like his own uncle, Abu Lahab, whom God cursed through a revelation, along with his wife. Worst of all was the leader of the Makhzum clan of the Quraysh, Abu Jahl. Abu Jahl made a mockery of Muhammad and confronted his followers. Abu Jahl would single out converted slaves and then have his hired thugs assault them. He would harass other Meccan Muslims in public, sometimes debarring them from markets, at other times excluding them from caravan trips.

Once Muhammad was established in Medina he had no choice but to fight the likes of Abu Jahl. God Himself had declared: 'Permission to fight is given to those on whom war is made.' (22:39) But it was always a defensive war. The war Muhammad waged against Mecca was not a struggle for prestige or wealth, but for the survival of God's Word and his own person. His helpers from Medina joined the migrants from Mecca. They provided the migrants with food and shelter, but their own resources were stretched to the limit. They began to raid the caravans of their Meccan foes. They raided only small caravans at first, and never attacked during those times when fighting, and especially blood feuds, were prohibited. As someone who had guided many a successful caravan, Muhammad knew the routes and the seasons. He also knew the wells where Meccan traders would pass with their camels and their goods.

In December 623, over a year after the beleaguered Muslims had fled to Medina, Muhammad ordered a small detachment to spy on a caravan to the south. It was travelling along the route to Yemen, at the oasis of Nakhlah that links Mecca to Taif. It was the last day of the holy month of Rajab, and Muhammad had ordered his followers not to attack, but they disobeyed. They killed some, took others captive and brought the caravan back to Medina. Muhammad was appalled. Not only had his followers disobeyed him; they had also desecrated a holy month. They had gone against God's Word. Since their actions mirrored his leadership, he was responsible. The prophet who had pledged to be a divine mediator had betrayed his own prophecy. He was riven with distress and prayed for guidance from above.

It came, like a fresh rain after the longest, driest drought of summer:

> They ask you about war in the holy month.
> Tell them:
> 'To fight in that month is a great sin.
> But a greater sin in the eyes of God is
> to hinder people from the way of God,
> and not to believe in Him,
> and to bar access to the Holy Mosque,
> and to turn people out of its precincts.
> And oppression is worse than killing.'

'And oppression is worse than killing.' He started to breathe a sigh of relief with these words, as the revelation continued:

> They will always seek war against you
> till they turn you away from your faith,
> if they can.
> But those of you who turn back on their faith
> and die disbelieving
> will have wasted their deeds
> in this world and the next.
> They are inmates of Hell,
> and abide there forever. (2:217)

The Almighty had replaced a general rule of high value with a general rule of higher value. Yes, killing is forbidden in the sacred month, but worse than killing is oppression, hindering people from the way of God.

Empowered by this Sign, Muhammad accepted the actions of his followers at Nakhlah. Taking the spoils of war, he divided them among the Muslims of Medina.

More war would follow. The provocation to his former tribesmen and townsmen was clearer than the desert sky. Muhammad and his followers braced themselves for the next outbreak in what was to become an unending conflict with their Meccan kinsmen and opponents. During the next nine years Muhammad planned thirty-eight battles that were fought by his fellow believers and he led twenty-five military campaigns himself. The merchant messenger had become a military strategist.

Muhammad did not have to wait long to lead his first full-scale military campaign. It came at the wells of Badr the following year, in 624, less than four months after the skirmish at Nakhlah. The Muslims planned to attack a caravan coming south from Palestine to Mecca. The Meccans learned of their plan, and met them with a force that far outnumbered the Muslim band. Muhammad and his followers should have lost; indeed, they would have lost, except for the intervention of angels. Appearing on their side was a heavenly host, a band of divine emissaries such as they had never seen before. The celestial warriors preceded their desert protégés. They watched over them. They bolstered them. They gained them a victory, as the Almighty attested in yet another Sign:

God helped you during Badr
at a time when you were helpless,
So act in compliance with the laws of God:
You may well be grateful.

Remember when you said to the faithful:
'Is it not sufficient that your Lord
should send for your help
3,000 angels from the heavens?'

Indeed, if you are patient and take heed for yourselves,
even though the enemy come rushing at you suddenly,
your Lord will send 5,000 angels.

And God did not do so
but as good tidings for you,
and to reassure your hearts –
For victory comes from God alone,
the Almighty, the All-knowing. (3:123–6)

The battle of Badr struck fear into the hearts of the Meccans, but it also made some resolve even more firmly to defeat the upstart Muslims. Among the Meccan opponents was Hind ibn Utbah, the wife of the mighty Meccan warrior Abu Sufyan. She had lost both her uncle and her father in the battle of Badr. She incited her husband, though he was both Muhammad's cousin and his foster-brother, to write verses against the Prophet and against the religion of Islam. It was Abu Sufyan's caravan the Muslims had tried to capture at

Badr. Though the Muslims had won the battle, they had lost the caravan. Soon after, Abu Sufyan, at his wife's insistence, began to plan the next encounter. By 625 he had assembled a huge army of foot soldiers and cavalry. He marched towards Medina. The Muslims countered by moving out of the city proper and engaged their rivals on the slopes of a nearby mountain, Uhud.

Despite the superior numbers of the Meccans, the battle went well for the Muslims until some of Muhammad's followers broke ranks too early, perhaps anticipating another victory such as Badr. It was not to be. The Meccans counterattacked, and Khalid ibn al-Walid, one of the brilliant Meccan nobles, led his squadron to the unprotected rear of the Muslim formation. Catching them unawares, he began a great slaughter. The Prophet's uncle Hamzah was felled by a skilled Meccan javelin thrower, and Muhammad himself, though protected by twenty of his closest followers, was knocked off his horse. One of his teeth was broken, his face gashed, a lip bruised. Abu Sufyan had even dared to hope that Muhammad might die from his wounds. When he began to taunt the defeated Muslim troops, Muhammad sent his trusted lieutenant, 'Umar, to give him the riposte: 'God is most high and most glorious,' shouted 'Umar. 'We are not equal: our dead are in paradise, yours in hell, and by God, you have not killed the Prophet. He is listening to us even as we speak!'

Not only was Muhammad listening but he also had resolved to learn the deeper lesson behind this bitter defeat. The defeat of Uhud became as important for Islam as the victory of Badr. The fate of Muslims is always in God's hands:

> He knows what lies between their hands and behind them.
> (2.255 partial [*Ayat al-Kursi* (the Throne Verse)])

In defeat as in victory the Muslims had to acknowledge that their fate was not theirs but God's to decide, as was revealed in this verse:

> God had already fulfilled
> the Divine promise to you when you were
> destroying them by His permission,
> until you weakened
> and argued over the order,
> and you disobeyed
> after He showed you what you desired.
> Some of you wanted this world,
> and some of wanted the hereafter.
> Then He diverted you from them to test you,
> but now He has pardoned you.
> God is Gracious to the believers. (3:152)

The aftermath of the battle of Uhud reinforced Muhammad's resolve to secure the loyalty of all his followers, both Muslims and the non-Muslims bound to him by treaty. There followed some difficult, often bloody purges of tribes near Medina, then a major battle in 627, the battle of the Trench. A

mighty Meccan army was again led by Abu Sufyan, the archi-
tect of the battle at Uhud. He had hoped to invade Medina, to
defeat and destroy all Muslims, but yet again God granted
Muslims victory. Fierce foes like Abu Sufyan and also the
fiery Khalid ibn al-Walid at last saw the truth of the Qur'an.
They embraced Islam, and became Muslims.

After the battle of the Trench, Muhammad tried to win
other hesitant Meccans over to the religion of Islam. He
engaged in a peaceful pilgrimage, contacted the Meccan leaders and assured them of his intention, concluding a ten-year
peace treaty at Hudaibiya in 628. Still some doubted him and
it was not until 629 that he and his followers were allowed to
re-enter their native city. At last all Muslims – those Meccans
who had emigrated to Medina, those Medinans who had
joined them, and other tribes who had become their allies,
then also submitted to God – were able to return to Mecca in a
peaceful pilgrimage.

This pilgrimage took place in January 630. The sight of the
returning Meccans melted the hearts of many who had been
their enemies, even though others feared that Muhammad
would take vengeance on them. Breaking custom, Muhammad forgave all but his bitterest enemies. In his compassion
he mirrored the Source of Compassion, and the Almighty
granted Muslims Mecca as their reclaimed home, the centre of
their life and faith as Muslims.

As the eleventh year of the *hijrah* began in 632 CE,
Muhammad undertook preparations for a Muslim campaign
into Syria. Before the army left Medina, the Prophet went to

the local cemetery to ask Divine forgiveness for the deceased. As he was praying, the pains began – fierce, intense, abdominal pains. He finished praying and, surviving the night, led dawn prayer the next day. But the pains did not stop and took his life in 632, fulfilling yet another of God's promises:

> Every soul must know the taste of death.
> Then you will be sent back to Us. (29:57)

## CHAPTER 3

# 'A'ishah: Muhammad's Wife and Custodian of His Memory

## 680 CE

Muhammad had been left bereft at the death of Khadijah, and a close friend advised him to remarry. He married two women at first, a widow named Sawdah, and a young daughter of one of his allies, 'A'ishah. Later Muhammad married other women, but in many ways 'A'ishah was the most significant of his wives after Khadijah.

'A'ishah was not just the youngest, she was also the most beautiful of the Prophet's wives. Her father, Abu Bakr, had been an early and prominent Muslim, and he himself became the First Caliph or Successor to Muhammad after his death in 632 CE. 'A'ishah was a mere child of nine years when she was given in marriage to the Prophet in 623 CE. She survived him by several decades, not dying until she was sixty-five. By that time she had become a prominent figure in the community of Medina, and her life's story became integral to events that defined both the reception of the Qur'an and the development of the young Muslim community.

'A'ishah was very intelligent, at once keenly observant and endowed with an exceptional memory. She remembered more than just the text of the Qur'an; she also knew more than most other Muslims about how and when and why the Qur'an was revealed. She witnessed and reminded others of the details of Muhammad's demeanour, from the smallest domestic encounters to the major public actions that shaped the Muslim community. It is thanks to this exceptional marriage, between a man near the end of his life and a woman still near the beginning of hers, that we know so much about both of them.

'A'ishah had more than a quick mind and accurate memory: she also had a sharp tongue and was not afraid to speak the truth unadorned with niceties. Whenever she bested someone else in argument, the Prophet would smile and say, 'She is the daughter of Abu Bakr!' A Companion once said, 'I have not seen anyone more eloquent than 'A'ishah.' During the Prophet's lifetime she used to sit with other women and pass on the knowledge that she had received from Muhammad. In the decades after his death she remained a source of knowledge and wisdom for both women and men. 'Whenever a report appeared doubtful to us,' noted one of the Companions of the Prophet, 'we asked 'A'ishah about it, and we always learned something from her about it.'

She preferred the honorific title, 'The Mother of the Believers'. It was a title of respect given to her and to all of the wives of the Prophet:

> The Prophet is closer to the believers
> than their own selves,
> and his wives are as their mothers. (33:6)

But with the title also came certain duties and expectations:

> O wives of the Prophet,
> if any of you are openly indecent,
> her penalty will be doubled,
> and that is easy for God.
>
> But any of you who is humble to
> God and God's messenger,
> And acts with integrity,
> her we will reward doubly;
> And we have prepared
> a generous provision for her.
>
> O wives of the Prophet,
> you are not like any other women.
> If you are conscientious,
> don't be so submissive in speech
> that those with sickness in their hearts
> conceive desire;
> but do speak in civil terms.
>
> And settle down in your homes,
> and don't show off in public
> as was done in the time of ignorance.

> Pray regularly, and give alms,
> and obey God and the messenger of God.
> For God only wishes
> to remove defilement from you,
> people of the house,
> purifying you.
>
> And remember what is recited
> to you in your houses
> from the Signs of God and wisdom;
> for God is Subtle, Aware. (33:30–34)

The 'wisdom' of God, referred to in Chapter 33:34 and elsewhere, is taken to be the exemplary profile of the Prophet. Every aspect of life – from birth to death and everything that happens in between – was seen by Muslims through the behaviour of Muhammad. It was this Prophetic standard of behaviour, the Sunnah, that 'A'ishah helped to preserve and protect. Once she was asked to describe the Prophet. He was 'the Qur'an walking', replied 'A'ishah, meaning that his behaviour was the Qur'an translated into action. She did all that she could to preserve both the written Qur'an and the walking Qur'an, memorizing its verses and understanding them. At the same time she knew and embodied the Sunnah. It was in large part due to her example that Hadith, or traditions or reports about the Prophet, became conjoined with the Qur'an. If the Qur'an were God's inalterable Word, then the

Sunnah as etched in Hadith became its complement and its extension.

But Muhammad's unique status also placed a special burden on 'A'ishah and his other wives. During his lifetime his Companions and other Muslims were expected to behave with respect and courtesy towards them. Targeted by the disbelievers and often molested by them, his wives wore the veil as a means of protection. They were also enjoined from marrying anyone else after his death:

> When you ask his wives
> for something that you need,
> ask them from behind a screen:
> that is purer for your hearts
> and their hearts.
> You have no right to annoy
> the Messenger of God
> or to marry his widows
> after his passing, ever;
> for that would be monstrous of you
> in the sight of God. (33:53)

'A'ishah maintained her purity but perilously because of the demands put upon her as the Prophet's youngest wife. During the course of her marriage to the Prophet Muhammad, the battles of Badr, Uhud and the Trench were fought. These were the three major battles against the Quraysh, the major tribe of Mecca who opposed him, and shifted the balance of power out of the hands of the Quraysh and into the hands of the Muslims. Although she was still very young, 'A'ishah participated in all three battles, bringing water for Muslim warriors and helping to look after the wounded. She witnessed life and she witnessed death – in the way of God as in the way of His opponents. She understood both, yet she affirmed life.

Often when the Prophet went to war, he would draw lots to take one of his wives with him. In 626 when he went to fight the Banu al-Mustaliq, the lot fell to 'A'ishah. She was thirteen years old. She accompanied the victorious Muslims, but on the way back to Medina, after a brief decampment, the Prophet unexpectedly ordered the army to continue the march back. 'A'ishah had stepped out of the litter and gone behind a dune to relieve herself. Noticing that her necklace was missing, she searched in the sand for it. She lost track of time, and when she finally returned to the camp, only its traces remained. So light was she that the men carrying her litter could not tell whether or not she was in it, and they had left without her. 'A'ishah sat down, waiting and hoping that someone would notice her absence and come back for her. No one did, but fortunately for her a young Muslim man who had fallen behind the army was trying to catch up when he reached the place where she had been left. He found 'A'ishah lying fast asleep. Waking her up, he had her climb on the back of his own camel. Then, leading the camel by the hand, he set off on foot after the army, hoping that they would soon catch up. They did, but not until later the next morning when the army had halted for a rest during the hottest part of the day. As luck would have it, some detractors had seen the two arrive together, unaccompanied. Gossip and slanderous lies began to spread. Eventually the story reached the Prophet. By then the whole community was talking about what might or might not have happened between the two young Muslims as they returned home from the battle against the Banu al-Mustaliq. The outcome of their 'affair' seemed more consequential than the outcome of the battle.

As a result of the gossip, the Prophet and his household came under great strain. No revelation came to clarify the matter. The Prophet, perhaps at the instigation of his cousin, 'Ali, questioned Barirah, 'A'ishah's maidservant. Had she detected anything amiss in 'A'ishah's behaviour? 'By Him who sent you with the truth,' replied Barirah, 'I have seen nothing wrong with her, other than that she is a young girl and sometimes she falls asleep while she is kneading the dough and a lamb comes along and eats it!' Some of the Companions who were present scolded Barirah. They prodded her to tell all that she knew. 'Glory be to God!' she replied. 'I know as much about her as a jeweller knows about a piece of pure gold!'

The Prophet then tried to vindicate 'A'ishah's honour in public. Summoning everyone to the mosque, he defended her reputation. But the detractors, those who had instigated the trouble, also came to the mosque and provoked arguments about what the Prophet meant. They almost came to blows over the matter. Finally the Prophet mounted the pulpit and, addressing the assembled believers, thundered: 'How does anyone dare to cast suspicion on the house of the Prophet of God?' He did not single out the accusers but made each of the tribes responsible for the conduct of its members. The one most adamant in defaming 'A'ishah's honour was handed over to his tribe to be punished by them. What had been a rumour mill became a matter of collective responsibility. Soon afterwards Gabriel revealed to the Prophet that 'A'ishah was indeed innocent:

> Those who put forth the lie
> Are a clique among you.
> Don't think it bad for you;
> No, it is better for you.
> Every one of them will get
> What he earned from the sin.
> And the one among them
> Who took it upon himself to puff it up
> Will have a tremendous punishment.
> When you heard it,
> Why didn't the faithful men and women
> Think the best on their own and say,
> 'This is an obvious lie!'?
>
> Why didn't they bring
> Four witnesses to testify to it?
> If they didn't produce witnesses,

Then *they* are the liars
In the sight of God…

Why didn't you say,
When you heard it,
'It is not for us
to talk about this.
By the glory of God,
This is serious slander!'?

God warns you not to revert
To anything like this ever,
If you are believers.

And God makes the Signs clear to you,
For God is all Knowing, supremely Wise. (24:11–18)


'God makes the Signs clear to you.' This condemnation of
slander occurs in the Chapter of Light. There is a lyrical hymn
to light in verses 35–40 but the light here is moral; it is a blaz-
ing white light directed at the detractors. It upholds the
honour of 'A'ishah but it also empowers women as well as
men to be responsible for their own fate: a lie should be called
a lie when it is an obvious untruth hurting the reputation of
other women.

The Affair of the Lie, above all, illustrates the crucial principle at stake in interpreting the Qur'an. Not all Signs are
general dicta. Some have specific historical contexts, which
illumine why certain verses were revealed, even as they set

forth moral standards incumbent on Muslims in every age and in every place.

After 626 no one could ignore the fact that 'A'ishah's honour and reputation had been protected by divine decree. From then on everyone became even more aware of her high station with God. For later codifiers of Islamic law, her embarrassment occasioned a very specific directive about false witnesses:

> As for those who accuse
> chaste women,
> but fail to produce four witnesses,
> whip them eighty lashes
> and never take testimony
> from them ever,
> for they are the ones
> who are immoral. (24:4)

Not only is the virtuous woman then restored to honour when her accusers fail to make their case but a heavy penalty falls on the false accusers: they forfeit their standing as devout Muslims. Worse than the marks of the lashes is the stigma of alienation from other Muslims. It never ceases; its sting lasts for ever.

Another lingering effect of the Affair of the Lie was its impact on 'A'ishah's relationship with 'Ali. 'Ali was among the family of the Prophet in a triple sense. Not only had he been with his cousin Muhammad since the earliest revelation, he had also fought in many of the major battles, and he had married Muhammad's oldest daughter by Khadijah. 'Ali was among Muhammad's most trusted confidants, and so it was natural that the Prophet would have asked him about 'A'ishah's dilemma. 'Ali is reported to have recommended questioning 'A'ishah's slave girl, Barirah, and even after Barirah defended 'A'ishah, 'Ali is said to have favoured divorcing her and marrying someone better. The ill will between them contributed to 'A'ishah's subsequent decision to side with two other Companions in opposing 'Ali as the Fourth Caliph after he had become embroiled in conflict with relatives of his predecessor, 'Uthman. The result of this was the battle of the Camel. Taking place in 656, it shaped the complex pattern of succession in Islam and opened the way to a new dynasty, the Umayyads, Meccan aristocrats linked to the Third Caliph, 'Uthman.

But even before the Affair of the Lie, with its ominous sequel, their age difference and family rivalry must have exacerbated the tension between 'Ali and 'A'ishah. 'Ali was younger than his cousin and father-in-law, Muhammad, but he was much older than 'A'ishah, as was his wife Fatimah. It seems likely that the marriage of Muhammad to 'A'ishah took place at almost the same time, in 623, as the marriage of 'Ali to Fatimah. Both women sought the affection of the Prophet, one as a child bride, the other as a doting daughter. 'A'ishah is said to have been jealous of Fatimah, as she was of 'Ali's deceased mother-in-law, Khadijah.

'Ali would have known the well-attested tradition about

'A'ishah's jealousy of Khadijah. 'A'ishah was childless, while Khadijah was not only the first Muslim but also the mother of the Prophet's children. One day, under duress from the unfavourable comparison made between her and Khadijah by other wives, 'A'ishah's sharp tongue got the better of her good judgement. She derided her predecessor as 'that toothless old woman whom God has replaced with a better'. Muhammad rebuked her. 'No, God has not replaced her with a better. She believed in me when I was rejected. When they called me a liar, she proclaimed me truthful. When I was poor, she shared with me her wealth, and God granted me her children, withholding those by other women!'

The irony of this tradition is that it is supported by an impeccable authority: 'A'ishah herself! 'A'ishah was honest, even when she was at fault. In other traditions that she reported, she vented her irritation with fellow wives, their jealousies and competition for the affection of a husband whose main concern was to be the faithful Prophet of God and the advocate of his community. 'A'ishah is said to have recorded more than 2,000 traditions of the Prophet. It is a prodigious feat matched by only three other Companions, none of whom was as close to the Prophet, or as jealous of his affection, as was 'A'ishah. To the extent that women's rights remain central to defining the ethos of Islam, 'A'ishah was a pioneer whose example continues to inspire Muslim women, and to elicit the respect of Muslim men.

CHAPTER 4

# The Dome of the Rock: Jerusalem Landmark, Qur'anic Icon

692 CE

The Dome of the Rock is a building encircling a rock in Jerusalem. It sits on a hill or mount known as the Noble Close and overlooks the entire span of nooks and crannies, streets and lanes, houses and markets that dot Jerusalem. It is the noblest emblem of the Noble Close in a city hallowed by memory and by devotion of Jews, Christians and Muslims, and it is to this city and to the rock inside the Dome of the Rock that Abraham came. On this rock Solomon built his temple and near the rock Jesus was buried. It is also from a place near this rock that Muhammad the Prophet ascended to Heaven on the Night Journey.

Muslims had conquered Jerusalem by 637, and they knew the history of the Temple Mount – as it was called after Solomon's temple was destroyed – yet they did not build the Dome of the Rock till 692. While it had been a proud moment for the second Caliph 'Umar ibn al-Khattab to have captured the holy city in the name of Islam in 637, his pride yielded to fear among his successors. They did not fear their military or political rivals but they were in awe of the architectural splendours of the Byzantine city. The newest followers of Abraham, the Muslims, lacked a structure to match either the memory of the ancient Jewish Temple or the beauty of the Byzantine Christian church of the Holy Sepulchre. Over half a century after the Muslim conquest of Jerusalem, the Umayyad Caliph 'Abd al-Malik, finally built on the Temple Mount. He erected a unique structure, employing architects and masons and calligraphers to tell the Qur'anic plan of revelation. It is a familiar story but with a different ending. The line of Abraham encompasses the descendants of Ishmael as well as Isaac. Just as the Unseen had marked Jews and Christians through their prophets, so now the Almighty One favoured Muslims through the dispensation to an Arab prophet, the last prophet, Muhammad.

The Dome of the Rock is near a mosque, the Furthest Mosque, where Muhammad is believed to have landed on his Night Journey, but it is not itself a mosque. It is actually a shrine that attests to the ascent of Muhammad on the Night Journey, although the actual place of ascent is marked by a smaller dome adjacent to it. The purpose of the Dome of the Rock is to highlight the great rock within its wondrous shape. There are two octagonal ambulatories that surround a circular centre, itself north of an immense artificial esplanade. The intention of the design is to enhance the message that it conveys in stone and script. Marking this space as hallowed are delicate mosaics. They in turn frame scroll upon scroll of Arabic letters, which are Signs from the Book. They project a message for all to see. It is the message of the Qur'an writ large upon these walls, mingling geometric forms with block-like letters. Letters expand to words, words combine into sentences, and all look down upon the rock, making the rock their mirror, even as they are its reflection.

The Signs transcend human signs, just as the Book transcends the scroll and pen that make and mark human books as merely human creations. These are Signs from the one Book that precedes all human books, the Protected Tablet:

> This is a Glorious Recitation
> (preserved) in a Protected Tablet. (85:21–2)

The same heavenly Book inspired the Torah, the Psalms and the Gospel. It is from the Book beyond all books that the Holy Qur'an was revealed. Its story comes in moments of announcement from the Archangel Gabriel to the Prophet Muhammad. Just as Gabriel had announced to Mary that she would be the mother of Jesus, so Gabriel announced again and again to Muhammad the story that would complete for him – and for Arabs, and for humankind – the message that had been given earlier to Jews and to Christians.

While the story is transcendent, it is not transparent. The most important Signs only appear after you enter the building. Looking up, you see the main text on the inner face of the arcade. You read the main text as you circumambulate the circular centre and before you return to where you entered.

The main text begins on the south side of the octagon with

part of the declaration of faith. It is followed by a series of excerpts from different parts of the Qur'an, interspersed with creedal dicta reinforcing its central message:

> In the Name of God, Full of Compassion, Ever
> Compassionate

> *There is no god but God. He is One. He has no associate.*

> To Him belongs sovereignty and to Him belongs praise.
> He gives life and He brings death;
> and He is Able to do all things. (64:1; 57:2)

> *Muhammad is the servant of God and His messenger*

> Lo! God and His angels bless the Prophet.
> O believers, invoke blessings on him,
> and greet him with a prayer for peace. (33:56)

> *The blessing of God be on him and peace be on him,*
> *and may God have mercy (on him)*

> O People of the Book,
> do not go to excess
> in your religion,
> and do not say of God
> anything but truth.
> The Messiah,
> Jesus son of Mary
> was only a Messenger of God.
> The Messiah,

and a Word of God
bestowed on Mary,
and a Spirit from God.
So believe in God,
and do not speak of a trinity;
it is best for you to refrain.
God alone is the One worthy of worship:
glory to God,
exalted beyond having a son.
To God belongs all
in the heavens and the earth;
and God is sufficient
to manage it all.

The Messiah
does not disdain
to be a servant of God,
and neither do the intimate angels.
As for those who disdain
the worship of God
and who aggrandize themselves,
God will gather
all of them up. (4:171–2)

*O God, bless Your messenger and Your servant Jesus son of Mary*

'Peace be upon me the day I was born,

and the day I die,
and the day I shall be raised alive!'

Such was Jesus, son of Mary,
a word of the truth concerning which they doubt.

It befits not (the Majesty of) God that He
should take unto Himself a son.

Glory be to Him!
When He decrees a thing,
He merely says to it: 'Be!'
and it is.

Lo! God is my Lord and your Lord.
So serve Him:
That is the straight path. (19:33–6)

God (Himself) is witness
that there is no God but Him.
And (so are) the angels
and those endowed with knowledge,
maintaining His creation in justice.
There is no god but He,
the Almighty, the Wise.

Lo! religion with God (is)
surrender (to His will and guidance).
Those to whom the Book was given

disagreed out of rivalry
only after knowledge came to them.
Whoever rejects the signs of God,
lo! God is swift at reckoning. (3:18–19)

And then, as you leave to the south after having circum-ambulated the rock, you absorb the message that Jesus indeed was the Messiah to be raised on high with God, but yet a servant, and not a son, of the One who is 'my Lord and your Lord'. And again you find other Signs that repeat and reinforce the same message:

In the Name of God, Full of Compassion, Ever
    Compassionate

*There is no god but God. He is One. He has no associate.*

Affirm: He is God the One,
God the Ceaseless.
Unbegetting and Birthless,
Like unto Him is no one. (112)

*Muhammad is the Messenger of God, the blessing of God be on him*

In the Name of God, Full of Compassion, Ever
    Compassionate

*There is no god but God. He is One. He has no associate.*
*Muhammad is the Messenger of God.*

Lo! God and His angels bless the Prophet:

O believers, invoke blessings on him,
And greet him with a prayer for peace. (33:56)

In the name of God, Full of Compassion, Ever Compassionate

*There is no god but God. He is One.*

Praise be to God,
Who has not begotten a son,
Nor has a partner in His dominion,
Nor has need of a protector due to abasement.
So magnify Him with the magnificence due Him! (17:111)

To Him belongs sovereignty and to Him belongs praise.
He gives life and He brings death;
and He is Able to do all things. (64:1; 57:2)

*Muhammad is the Messenger of God. The blessing of God be on him.*

*The Servant of God, the Blessed Leader, the Commander of the*
    *Faithful,*
*built this dome in the year two and seventy. May God accept it*
    *from him*
*and be content with him! Amen! Praise be to God, Lord of all*
    *worlds! (1:2)*
*The Servant of God, the Blessed Leader, the Commander of the*
    *Faithful,*

The last phrase, which is an inscription, may seem obscure. The date 'two and seventy' is 72 AH, referring to anno hijrae, the Muslim calendar date, which corresponds to 692 CE.

Similarly, the Umayyad Caliph is referring to himself by his titles ('servant', 'leader', 'commander') rather than by his actual name, 'Abd al-Malik.

But apart from these explanations, how do the Qur'anic Signs from the Dome of the Rock project its message? They are repeated, but repetition is only for the sake of clarity and emphasis. Verses and dicta are repeated to instruct; each accent counts, each underscores an insistent message. On the inner face of the octagon the declaration of faith is followed by conflated verses describing the powers of God. The Prophet Muhammad is introduced with a blessing that echoes the Qur'an even though it does not directly quote from the Qur'an.

What follows is an exhortation to Christians, extolling Jesus also as a prophet but only a prophet: like all prophets and all men, he was mortal. The only eternal self-sufficient force is God Almighty. And the message of His Lofty Singleness comes in the form of a command to bend to His will, with the reminder that

> Whoever rejects the Signs of God,
> Lo! God is swift at reckoning. (3:19)

The inscription on the outer face consists of six sections set apart by ornaments, the last being the actual foundation notice. Each of the other five sections begins with the *basmalah*, perhaps to echo the pattern of the five daily prayers that was vouchsafed to Muhammad on the Night Journey in his exchange with Gabriel before the Celestial Throne. In each

of the first four sections, the prayer is followed by the statement of faith and a Qur'anic verse arrayed in such a way as to
form a self-contained and coherent statement, capped by a
blessing on the Prophet. The fifth and final section is stark: it is
merely the statement of faith with a blessing for Muhammad
and no further petition. Each of these sections on the outer
face in effect becomes a shorthand memo, a Sign encapsulat-
ing the major themes of the longer inscription on the inner
face.

What are we to make of the form of these Qur'anic quotes
that expand the actual Qur'anic text with other dicta? On the
one hand, Muslims from the time of the Third Caliph
'Uthman had established the standard literary version of A
Book of Signs. It has persisted unchanged throughout the centuries. But side by side with the literary text is a tradition of
drawing upon that text for a variety of rhetorical purposes.
The creative use of familiar scriptural associations amplifies
the text; it does not challenge it or change it. By the end of the
seventh century both listeners and readers would have
understood the Qur'an to be the core text adorning the Dome
of the Rock. A Book of Signs reflected the consensus of the
Muslim community. Its very existence confirmed and reinforced the power of that consensus. All agreed on the shape,
the content and the authority of that Book.

Ironically, since written copies of the Qur'an have not survived from the seventh century, the Dome of the Rock writ in
stone remains the earliest surviving Qur'anic text. Its inscriptions are best seen as commentaries addressed to an audience

that could be expected to understand the allusions to Jesus as signposts to 'the Unseen' God. To Muslims they are examples of the ultimate Truth, but to non-Muslims, whether Jews or Christians, they pose a challenge. They begin a Muslim version of scriptural proof-texting that grew and grew over centuries. As numerous parties turned to the Qur'an, they explored new and numerous ways to mine its content. Whether for proselytizing or for polemics, for prayer or for refutation, Muslims tried to engage its message creatively. To their opponents it may have seemed that they were projecting their own interests onto Divine intent, but in their minds the Qur'an announced a new standard of one Revelation to which they were pledged to be faithful as 'those who believe and do good deeds' (103:3 passim).

# Early Commentaries

## CHAPTER 5

# Ja'far as-Sadiq:
# Shi'ite Imam and
# Qur'anic Exegete

760 CE

Ja'far was an early interpreter of the Qur'an. He was an Imam, one endowed with divine authority. His authority was, above all, conferred through his bloodline. It was a bloodline unlike that of anyone else in the history of Islam.

Until very recently blood descent mattered in most societies. It determined life options. A sacred lineage conferred moral authority. Europeans used to call it *beata stirps*, holy roots that nourish and define the person blessed to have them.

Among Muslims, the line of those who traced themselves to the Prophet Muhammad through his daughter Fatimah and her husband 'Ali were thought to have the authority of both kings and saints. They were especially blessed from birth by virtue of their parentage. After Fatimah the line was patrilineal. It began with 'Ali, the cousin, playmate, devout follower, fellow warrior, then son-in-law of the Prophet Muhammad. 'Ali became the first Imam of Shi'ite Islam. 'Ali had two sons, Hasan and Husayn. The Prophet's grandsons and therefore his closest male heirs, they became the second and third Imams. The principal Shi'ite lineage continued through the offspring of Husayn, despite the latter's martyrdom in the notorious battle of Karbala that took place in 680. Ja'far as-Sadiq became the sixth Imam. He was the great-grandson of Husayn, and also one of the designated successors to 'Ali, his great-great grandfather, but his *beata stirps* ran even deeper. Ja'far as-Sadiq was not only one of the People of the Prophet's Household (*ahl al-bayt*), he also had another lineage that linked him back to the Prophet's generation. He was descended from both 'A'ishah, the Prophet's favourite wife after Khadijah, and from Fatimah, Khadijah and Muhammad's oldest daughter as well as 'Ali's wife.

Imams rely on lineage but they also depend on character. Ja'far is known as as-Sadiq or the Truthful One because it was his dedication to truth that made him the most important of the Shi'ite Imams after 'Ali and 'Ali's younger son, the martyr Husayn.

None of this complex genealogical reckoning would matter had Ja'far not also been an exceptional scholar. His learning was prodigious. He lived and taught in Medina at a time when Sunnis and Shi'ites had different views but were not yet competing camps within the Muslim community. Among his students were Abu Hanifa and Malik ibn Anas, who became founders of two of the four Sunni schools of law. Malik ibn Anas leaves no doubt about the close friendship that existed between him and Ja'far as-Sadiq. Their collaboration helped shape Islamic norms and values for all periods, and it also suggests the fluidity of the lines between the two major groups defining Islam in the second *hijri* or Muslim century. Sunnis accepted the history of the Muslim community or *ummah*, as it had unfolded: all the Righteous Caliphs were indeed righteous, while Shi'ites saw that history differently. 'Ali was the most righteous of the Righteous Caliphs. Indeed, the other Caliphs, but especially his immediate predecessor 'Uthman, were less righteous because they did not defer to 'Ali. 'Ali's delayed caliphate and even more the martyrdom of his son Husayn, represented, for Shi'ites, a betrayal of the ideals of the earliest Muslim community. The Shi'ites preferred their Imams, who lacked political power, to the Caliphs, who exercised political power.

There was no full-scale cleavage between Sunnis and Shi'ites until the 'Abbasid revolution. The 'Abbasids revolted against the Umayyads in 747 CE with support from proto-Shi'ites, that is, those who were linked to the Prophet's family and to the memories of 'Ali and his martyred son, Husayn. Even after the 'Abbasids came to power and established Kufa as their new capital, other branches of the Prophet's household continued to protest. Some revolted against 'Abbasid rule, just as their predecessors had earlier revolted against Umayyad rule. Yet Ja'far as-Sadiq neither joined them nor supported their cause. He preferred to be an academic luminary and a political quietist. Throughout the early 750s, he maintained the stay-at-home policy of his father. Living in Medina, he did not pose an immediate threat to the 'Abbasid Caliph in Kufa and was left alone.

However, in 753 CE, a new 'Abbasid Caliph came to power.

Al-Mansur was intent on securing his rule. He tried to use the intellectual elite, including Ja'far, to establish a theocratic state with himself as the viceregent of God. He also justified the rights of his family to the Caliphate by referring to his blood-line. Even though it was not as strong as Ja'far's, he claimed that he and his offspring, since they were direct descendants of the Prophet's uncle, 'Abbas, had equal claim to the Imamate. In 760 al-Mansur proclaimed himself the Imam-Caliph.

This double claim was too much for Ja'far to bear. As the designated Imam of his generation, he had to oppose the Caliph on two grounds. First, according to the Shi'ite notion of authority and succession, the Imamate must remain distinct from the Caliphate until such time as God would make an Imam victorious. Second, the Imam can only be a person descended from the Prophet through his daughter Fatimah. The Imam derives his exclusive authority, not by political claims but by *explicit* designation from the previous Imam. He also inherits a special inner knowledge or *'ilm*, passed down through holy blood from generation to generation.

Still, Ja'far's opposition took not a political path but an intellectual path that wove itself through the Qur'an. By 760 Ja'far had become more than just an elder statesman for the *ahl al-bayt*. He was a respected Qur'anic scholar. Some claim that he actually wrote a commentary on the Qur'an. While it has not survived, one can easily gauge some of its principal points by consulting later commentaries written by Shi'ite scholars. Ja'far offered a threefold view of the Qur'an. The first and most obvious reading was literal. One could read the text in Arabic. By the time of Ja'far, however, much of the language of the Qur'an was not the same as everyday Arabic, and so one aspect of interpretation was to translate Qur'anic Arabic into vernacular Arabic. But more than translation was necessary to understand the context of verses, chapters and themes from A Book of Signs. That second level of interpretation was historical. It required understanding the circumstances of the time of the Prophet and the first Muslims. Of course, it also meant understanding the events that determined a line of succession that bypassed the *ahl al-bayt* and instead fell to the Prophet's close companions: Abu Bakr, 'Umar and 'Uthman. Together with 'Ali, these three were known as the Righteous Caliphs, but their righteousness had to be re-evaluated in the light of 'Ali's moral superiority. The third level went further still. Going beyond both language and history, it explored the realm of imagination, of myth, of intuition. Some have called it the allegorical approach to the Qur'an. It was the most tortuous and least accessible way to experience the mysteries of A Book of Signs.

Yet this third way, the allegorical way, offered the most creative, and open-ended, of all the ways to engage the Noble Qur'an. Ja'far was especially adept at the second and the third, even though it was often difficult to distinguish between them. 'Ali, for instance, due to this close relationship with Muhammad, must have been present at some of the revelations that became A Book of Signs or The Noble Qur'an. Lacking explicit mention of 'Ali in the Qur'anic revelations, how can one detect indirect references to him and also to his family? This was a question that motivated much of Imam Ja'far's effort to make sense of A Book of Signs. Like other descendants of the House of the Prophet (*ahl al-bayt*) who became known as Shi'ites, or partisans of 'Ali, he distinguished between clear and ambiguous verses. As the Imam of the time, Ja'far as-Sadiq was respected as the most authoritative source of that knowledge which includes esoteric as well as evident meanings of the Qur'an. He could move deftly between clear verses in which there is no room for demurral or difference in their interpretation, and other, ambiguous verses that require multi-levelled interpretation and often evoke disagreement, even among believers.

Like Tabari in the tenth century, Imam Ja'far prized the clear verses: any believer should be able to comprehend their meaning. However, unlike Tabari, he ascribed still greater importance to the ambiguous verses. These, in Imam Ja'far's view, were the verses where the meaning is not clear except to those who have the authority to interpret them, namely, the Imams. 'Ali, for instance, is said to have declared that no less than one quarter of the Qur'an is about the Imams. The Imams are the Truthful Ones (9:119) and the possessors of knowledge (3.6). They are also those linked to the People of Remembrance (16:43–4) and to the Party of God (*hizbullah*; 5:56). It is they who are the Family of the Prophet:

> This is the good news that God gives to
> His servants who believe and do good works;

> Say: 'I ask no reward from you for this,
> Only the affection due to (my) kin.' (42:23)

Among other verses allegorically referring to the Imams are:

- The Signs of God – 'Only the unbelievers would deny Our signs' (29:49); each Imam is taken to be a Sign of God (*ayatullah*). (7:9; 10:7; 22:57; 38:29)
- The Straight Path becomes the Way designated by the Imams. (1:6, but also 6:153, 15:41, 16:76, 20:135, 43:42)
- The Bounty of God (14:28–9) is the Imams and they are also the Cord of God (3:103) as well as the Firmest Handle (2:256).
- The Light of God is especially important, since it designates not just the Imams but also their quasi-divine character.

> Then believe in God and His messenger
> And the light that He has sent down. (64:8)

While Sunni Muslims would dispute all these references, it is the last reference, connecting the Imams to light, that provokes the sharpest difference. It projects not just a different notion of the Imams but also of the Prophet. Muhammad was said to be but a man, as were all the prophets before him and all the successors or Caliphs after him. Yet Chapter 64:8 is the *locus classicus*, the most famous text, for identifying both Muhammad and the Imams with the Light of God (although there are also several other verses, such as 4:174, 6:122, 7:157, 9:32, 24:36, 57:28 and 66:8.)

Despite the quiescent nature of Ja'far's opposition to the Caliph, his teaching, and especially the exclusive authority he ascribed to himself as an interpreter of the Qur'an, undermined the claims of al-Mansur. The Caliph had Ja'far arrested and brought to Samarra, where he was kept under supervision. After a few years al-Mansur allowed Ja'far to return to Medina, but then sent the governor of Medina instructions to poison him. In 765 Imam Ja'far as-Sadiq died, and was buried in Jannat al-Baqi (the Garden of the Eternal) in Medina. His pre-eminence among Shi'ite, as also Sufi or mystical, Qur'an interpreters persists up to the present day, even though Saudi claiments to Medina, aghast at tomb cults focused on saints and Imams, destroyed Jannat al-Baqi in the early decades of the twentieth century.

## CHAPTER 6

# Abu Ja'far at-Tabari: Sunni Historian and Qur'anic Exegete

## 913 CE

Abu Ja'far Muhammad ibn Jarir at-Tabari (hereafter Tabari) was a Persian born in the mid-ninth century in what is today northern Iran. Though he did not die till 923 CE, he had already lived a long, productive life at the dawn of the fourth Muslim century. He was perhaps seventy-five years old when the Muslim calendar, which is lunar and not solar, and begins with the Prophet Muhammad's flight (*hijrah*) from Mecca to Medina, turned to a new century, in 913 CE. Like other devout non-Arab Muslims who aspired to be scholars, he had mastered Arabic as a second language. He knew Arabic but he did not think like his Arab co-religionists. He approached the entire period of Muslim history not as an Arab linked to western Arabia, the Prophet's birthplace, but as a Persian linked to Iran and to Mesopotamia, regions adjacent to Arabia and often in competition with it for local prestige among Muslims.

Tabari was aware that learning meant mastery of skills in rhetoric, grammar, syntax and eloquence. It also meant acknowledging the weight of the Muslim past, the figures who had been linked to the Prophet Muhammad and who were repositories of his message. First were the Qur'an reciters. They had preserved the book as a living oral source. Custodians of revelation, they made A Book of Signs their primary focus. In Tabari's era there were seven, or perhaps ten, or even fourteen different forms of both reading and reciting the Qur'anic text.

Beyond reciting the Qur'an and delighting in Arabic verse, Muslim scholars also needed to synthesize the streams of revelation and prophetic experience into systems of virtue, codes of conduct that could guide the emerging Muslim community. The people who did this were known as jurists. Two of them Tabari especially admired. One was Shafi'i who had died a hundred years earlier. Shafi'i had lived and written on the cusp of the third century of the Muslim era: he died in 820 CE, corresponding to 204 AH. He had been devoted to interpreting the Qur'an through the example of the Prophet, so much so that he had argued that the two sources of truth could not be in conflict: what the Qur'an announced the Prophet had lived, what he lived complemented and completed what the Qur'an announced. There could be no disagreement, much less conflict, between the Message and the Messenger. Another jurist, contemporary with Tabari, was Ahmad ibn Hanbal. Tabari admired Ibn Hanbal, but less for his juridical insight than for his prodigious command of reports about the Prophet, the helter-skelter mass of accounts that all claimed to be linked to the Prophet but depended on honourable, honest transmitters, for the authenticity of their content.

Sharing with Shafi'i the view that the Prophet's life and words completed the message of the Qur'an, Tabari followed Ibn Hanbal to Baghdad, the capital of the vast Islamic empire. There Tabari found some traditions or Prophetic tributes, but he also found that most of the links to pronouncements by or about the Prophet were outside Iraq. He travelled to Syria, to Egypt, to other towns in Iraq in order to gather material about the Prophetic legacy. He confirmed what he could, but he also rejected much of what he heard as spurious. At the same time he explored all aspects of the Islamic past. He engaged in contests for reciting Arabic poetry, drawing on verses that predated the rise of Islam. He discussed issues of Qur'an recitation: which forms were preferred? In which regions were they preferred, and by whom?

Tabari made his life's work the endeavour to summarize all that was known and all that he could discover about interpretations of A Book of Signs. He also wrote a vast history of the world, which some would argue has been as influential as his study of the Qur'an. If he had only written about the Qur'an he would still have been one of the most important Muslim scholars of all time. His body of work contained no less than thirty books and fills twelve volumes in a recent printed edition. Tabari surveyed all the work of his predecessors, aiming not so much to provide an order for the Signs as to enumerate and evaluate all possible approaches to them.

For Tabari, it was futile to try to imagine how the Prophet Muhammad received the stream of light from beyond. The Qur'an was a many-splendoured entity: it was a poem, a prayer book, a song, and also a code of laws. It was a poem because of its lyrical style and evocative words, but it was a poem unlike any other poem. The Qur'an was a prayer book because all Muslims used it for ritual prayer (*salat*) but also for invocatory prayer (*du'a*). Its recitation was musical but not like other songs: it conveyed meaning through sound. The Qur'an also had become a code of laws, in no small part due to the skill of devout Muslim jurists such as Shafi'i and Ibn Hanbal.

The Qur'an for Tabari was, above all, a further stage of revelation that had already been reflected in the Bible. The Qur'an, in his view, was the Bible multiplied since it contained so many of the stories familiar to Jews and Christians but with new accents. Much shorter than the Torah of Jews, the Qur'an is bigger than the Christian Gospel(s). Although Muhammad produced no miracle, yet the Qur'an was a Divine miracle that he transmitted. Time and again the task of the interpreter was to demonstrate how the revelations given to Muhammad fulfilled earlier prophecies, while also surpassing them in scope, accuracy and insight.

One of the first instances of Tabari's distinctive approach appears in his interpretation of the Opening Chapter. The final verses read:

> Guide us to the path of True Direction,
> The path of those whom You favour,
> Not of those who cause You anger,
> Nor of those who took to the path of deviation. (1:6–7)

In imitation of Socratic dialogue, he has an anonymous ques-
tioner ask him his opinion about the party who caused anger,
and the party who took to the path of deviation.

Tabari responds: 'Those who cause divine anger are those
whom God describes in His Revelation' as:

> Those whom God cursed
> and at whom God was wrathful,
> and of whom God made apes and swine,
> and who worshipped idols –
> that is the worse, in actuality,
> and further astray from the right way. (5:60)

In other words, Tabari interpreted the Qur'an in terms set by
the Qur'an. Looking at the Opening Chapter, the seven verses
that became the prototype for all revelations in A Book of
Signs were interpreted by Tabari by looking at a subsequent
chapter, 'The Table,' where the same Arabic words were used
for 'wrath' and 'straying'. In this second case it seems to be the
Jews who suffered both God's anger and lost their way or
went astray. Tabari then confirms the identity of this group by
citing numerous pages from Traditions of the Prophet
Muhammad (the Hadith) that name the Jews as those with
whom God is indignant.

Later he notes that the second half of the declamation
could also refer to a second group. While it might seem that
those with whom God is angry were also the same as those
who had gone astray, there could, in fact, be another group,

one differentiated and marked by having gone astray. These could be Christians, as seems apparent later in the Chapter of the Table when God commands:

> People of the Book,
> do not exceed the bounds of truth in your religion,
> and follow not the whims of a people who went astray
> before,
> and led many astray.
> and now again have gone astray from the right way. (5:77)

To one who reads Tabari's commentary on the final verses of the Opening Chapter and stops here, it would seem that he is openly anti-Jewish and anti-Christian, parading Islam as the only true religion at the expense of its two predecessors, Judaism and Christianity. Yet an openly polemical reading of his commentary is qualified by what follows. In every section of his Commentary, Tabari quotes commentaries that others before him have offered, and summarizes their views before giving his own. It is not until the end that Tabari suggests what might be the 'real' meaning of particular verses.

Tabari begins with a rhetorical query: why has the Almighty made such a long delivery in the very first Chapter? Didn't the initial verses, lauding God as Compassion and Compassionate, as Lord of all Creation, as Master of the Day of Determination, didn't those two verses suffice? 'What more wisdom is there', asks Tabari, 'in the five other verses apart from that which is already contained in the first two?'

That rhetorical question then allows Tabari to restate the Divine intent. It was, above all, to confirm the Divine origin of the Qur'an. Its form matches its content. Even as it affirms previous scriptures, A Book of Signs is distinguished from previous scriptures by its marvellous order, its extraordinary coherence and the unique pattern of its composition.

Though imitators are legion, they are all defeated in trying to equal it. Orators cannot match the orderly arrangement of even its shortest chapters. Rhetoricians exhaust themselves trying to describe the form of even a part of it. Poets are baffled, and defeated, by its internal sounds that exceed all rules of verse.

As for intellectuals, they are the ones whose skills, in Tabari's view, are most pitiable in their approach to A Book of Signs. All they can do is submit and affirm that it comes from the Great One, the Vanquisher. It contains meanings not assembled in any other book brought down from Heaven to Earth. Through narrative, dialectics and parables, it offers imperatives to act and imperatives to refrain from acting, passages that attract and passages that frighten.

Uppermost in Tabari's mind is the ethical power of discourse. A Book of Signs, above all, demonstrates the Divine intent through passages that attract and passages that frighten. And that intent is illustrated nowhere more clearly than in the last two verses of the Opening Chapter. They serve a general purpose not restricted to Jews and Christians. 'Through mentioning in it the exemplary retribution He brought down on those who disobeyed Him, and the punishment which befell those who went against His command, His intent was to cause His servants to fear perpetrating acts of disobedience to Him and exposing themselves to His anger.' In other words, Jews and Christians were representative of all human beings, including Muslims, who might not comply with the Divine Will and so fail to pursue the straight path.

Tabari provides a more universal reading of not just the Opening Chapter but the entire Qur'an. He focuses, above all, on seeing Muhammad as the final Prophet who is nothing less than the successor and confirmation of Abraham. It is the saga of the Prophet Abraham that informs what happened to the Prophet Muhammad. Abraham progressed from ignorance and innocence (6:77–8) to uncertainty (2:260) and finally to faith in the One God, Full of Compassion, Ever Compassionate. It was Abraham who marked the journey from ignorance to prophecy, idolatry to oneness. He became the recipient of a Divine blessing for all humankind, and he made Arabia the place of his true descendants, those whose seed flowed from his concubine Hagar to her son Ishmael and then to all the Arabs, including those of the tribe of Quraysh into which the Prophet Muhammad was born.

And so while the Quraysh in particular and Arabs in general were privileged by Divine grace, grace was no more exclusively theirs than anger and punishment were the expected and probable outcome for all Jews and Christians. The Divine favour had touched both Jews and Christians, as several Qur'anic passages attest. In the same vein, suggests Tabari, it also flowed not just to Arab Muslims but also to

Persians who joined the Muslim fold after the Arab conquest of Iraq and Iran.

Although Tabari was a Persian and read the Qur'an, in part, as a Persian, he was also the product of his age. By the end of the third century in the *hijri* calendar, Islamic learning was no longer new, but it was also far from fixed as a form of observance and guidance for devout Muslims. Tabari seems to have harboured a sense of how the vast rivulets of scholarship that preceded him were turning into an ocean of interpretation that could confuse as well as inform. How does one provide a criterion for assessing the ocean of meaning within the Noble Qur'an? Tabari thought it necessary to divide all the Signs into three categories. There was one set of Signs for which the Prophet Muhammad, and he alone, was the interpreter (16.44 and 64). Another set of verses were those for which God, and God alone, could be the interpreter, such as verses indicating the Final Hour of Judgement, knowledge which even the Prophet did not know (7.187). And then there were the vast majority of verses; those that everyone who knew the Arabic language of the Qur'an could interpret.

Tabari had titled his great work *The Comprehensive Exposition of the Interpretation of the Verses of the Qur'an*. The word for 'interpretation' in Arabic was *ta'wil*, literally going back to first principles, trying to explain the Qur'an through the Qur'an. For him, *ta'wil* seemed identical with another word, *tafsir*, that is, expositing the meaning of words, phrases and passages from the Qur'an. In Tabari's mind, the two words flowed together like two tributaries of water; they were synonyms, if not homonyms, of the same enterprise.

The value of looking at first principles is the benefit of seeing God, the Prophet, and the 'ordinary' believer, as joint participants in the Qur'an. Precisely because there are two human 'readers', there must also be two levels of interpretation. The Prophet interpreted the Qur'an throughout his life; both his deeds and his words offer a 'reading' of its message. But for the ordinary believer, it is necessary to distinguish between the Signs, as not all have the same value. A Book of Signs contains Signs whose meaning the reader, with the proper background, can readily decipher. Their meaning should be transparent. Tabari calls these Clear Signs but there are others – the ones to which God alone knows the interpretation – that are Ambiguous Signs.

It is a clever distinction, especially in what it does not say. It does not say that the Clear Signs have only one possible interpretation; only that the levels of interpretation should be clear to one who approaches them with the proper background and intent. Nor are the Ambiguous Signs excluded from any human interpretation. They include the mysterious letters that introduce some of the Qur'anic Chapters, beginning with Chapter 2, the Chapter of the Cow, which after the *basmalah* has three letters: *alif, lam, mim*. By the time of Tabari, many Muslims had begun to consult the letters in Chapter 2 and later Chapters for auguries. A whole informal science of divination based on matching numbers with letters had emerged. Tabari condemned such interpretations of the

Ambiguous Signs, but at the same time, since everything in the Qur'an has both a purpose and a meaning, Tabari argued that one can understand these Ambiguous Signs. It is simply that one must delay trying to understand them until one has mastered the Clear Signs. In other words, each interpreter must first make sense of those Clear Signs, with their explicit spiritual and moral road maps, before veering into the more dangerous terrain marked by Ambiguous Signs.

Tabari's role as a Qur'an commentator was complicated by his own status as a Sunni Muslim. While he upheld the special virtue of 'Ali and all those linked to the Prophet's Household, he was committed to the path of political succession that produced first the Umayyad, then the 'Abbasid Caliphate. The degree to which Tabari represents a Sunni rather than a Shi'ite approach to the Qur'an can be seen in his cautious use of the term *ta'wil*. As we have seen before, he makes *ta'wil* equivalent to the more frequent and familiar word, *tafsir*. That may seem like a concession to Shi'ite sensibilities, but the category which Tabari highlights as Ambiguous Signs is more restricted for him than for his Shi'ite counterparts: it applies to the mysterious letters, and a few other passages, but not to one quarter of the Qur'an, as 'Ali is alleged to have said it does. Nor does it extend to the many verses that Shi'ites claimed had a meaning reserved for the Prophet's Household, especially for the Imams, the lineage of Shi'ite leaders, descended from 'Ali and Fatimah, the Prophet's daughter. For Tabari, Abu Bakr and 'Umar, as well as 'Ali, had sound credentials to be legitimate heirs, and therefore successors, to the Prophet Muhammad. Even 'Uthman could be accepted, if less enthusiastically than others, in the Sunni lineage known as the Righteous Caliphate.

Tabari has been the backstop for the dominant Sunni perspective on Qur'an interpretation. He lauded the Qur'an but as a text of Divine origin that required human responsibility in its interpretation. There is no special advance knowledge given to human beings by birth. Each person has to learn the words of the Qur'an, memorize its chapters, reflect on its message and then live by its Signs. The Shi'ite perspective was not just an alternative way of reading the text; it was unacceptable, flawed in its assumptions and injurious in its consequences.

# Later Interpretations

## CHAPTER 7

# Robert of Ketton: Polymath Translator of the Qur'an

## 1144 CE

Translation is hard work, never more so than when translating a scripture from its original language into another. To ponder the meaning of esoteric words is to explore the signs of other realities and then render them into their lyrical equivalents. Translators must know that other language – its grammar, its rhetoric, its ambivalences – as they know their own. That is the challenge faced by all foragers of the foreign, those who enter into others' mental space with the intent of linking it to their own.

To move from Latin to Arabic is to move from a language with all its antecedents in city life, where roads and houses, irrigation and water tanks, armies and taxes matter most, to a desert life, where tribes are the norm, spaces open, oases the lifeline for survival, and cities but dots etched on emptiness. It is not just that Latin and Arabic have different alphabets and grammars; they also reflect histories and societies even more disparate than their speech and writing.

How then can one hope to translate from Qur'anic Arabic,

the quintessential language of the desert, into High Latin, the expressive language of medieval cosmopolitan culture? This form of translation is perhaps the hardest work. It bridges world-views as well as linguistic patterns and social conventions.

For an educated twelfth-century Englishman, proficiency in Latin was natural. Robert of Ketton studied Latin because it was the language of both theology and science. But, thanks to Augustine and Jerome, Latin was more advanced in theology than it was in science. The rudiments of mathematics and astronomy were just becoming known in twelfth-century Europe. They became better known thanks to translations from Arabic into Latin coming out of southern Spain or Andalusia. Cities like Seville and Cordoba remained both Muslim and Arab, while cities that had been recaptured by Castillian Christians, like Badajoz and Toledo, retained links to their Andalusian past. Since the tenth century, scholars of philosophy and the sciences had been working with translations from Greek to Syriac, then to Arabic and now to Latin.

It was to Barcelona that Robert first went, in 1136. There he studied Arabic with Plato of Tivoli before finding the employment he sought, one that gave him the most satisfaction, and much-needed remuneration: translating scientific works in astronomy and geometry and especially algebra. He belonged to a school of translators, known from their location in that medieval centre of cosmopolitan life, Toledo.

Toledan translators were part of a Catholic Christian society that was not neutral about Islam. Hand in hand with converting ancient Greek wisdom into medieval European science was the desire to convert Muslims into Christians. In 1142, when the Abbot of Cluny, Peter the Venerable, visited Toledo, he asked Robert of Ketton to lead a team project. The goal was to produce the first Latin version of the Holy Qur'an. Well, not exactly 'Holy' since in the eyes of both Robert and his patron Peter, Muhammad was a charlatan rather than a true Prophet, and the book he produced less than a divine decree. Robert had tried his hand once before at religious Arabic. He had produced an anthology of essays about Muhammad in Latin, entitled *Saracen Fables or Lies and Ridiculous Tales from the Saracens*. This new undertaking – to translate A Book of Signs – also expressed contempt for its human subject in its title: 'The Law of the Pseudo-Prophet Muhammad'.

Consider the time of this undertaking. It was a time of warfare between Christians and Muslims. The First Crusade ended when Jerusalem was seized on behalf of the Pope in 1099. Less than fifty years later, Turkish/Muslim forces regrouped, and soon after Robert's translation was completed, the Turks took Edessa, in 1144. There then followed the Second Crusade (1147–9), and the Third Crusade (1189–92). All had papal approval. Christian support was marshalled against a Muslim adversary. Throughout the twelfth and into the thirteenth century European Christendom had a double mission: to slay Muslims and to retake Christian lands occupied by infidel Moors.

In such a charged atmosphere, the effort to 'honour' the pseudo-prophet of Islam by translating his lies (the Qur'an) was itself an ecumenical act. Peter the Venerable was more than Robert's patron; he also spurred the Christian initiative to understand, rather than vilify, Islam. While Peter wanted to expose the falsehood of the Qur'an, he also believed that one needed information about its content before confronting – and defeating – Muslim adversaries. Peter advocated battle by the pen rather than by the sword, even at a time when the Crusader mentality was on the ascendant. It may seem that most European Christians, including the Pope, had already made up their mind about the evil of Islam and the falsehood of the Qur'an. Peter suggests as much when he calls (in vain) for Islam to be approached, not 'as our people often do, by arms, but by words; not by force, but by reason; not in hatred, but in love'.

Yet the process of translation had consequences. The translation did find an audience; it was copied into numerous manuscripts, and then when the printing press became available in the sixteenth century, not only was the Gutenberg Bible published but also two Latin editions of Robert of Ketton's translation of the Qur'an. Blind hatred may not have been entirely replaced by enlightened engagement but at least a version of the Qur'an was available in a European language and some were trying to make sense of its signs.

Translating the Qur'an posed a challenge, above all, to Robert's imagination. It was a challenge of a different order than translating scientific texts from Arabic into Latin: scientific Arabic was not the same as Qur'anic Arabic. The former was a language that had been developed after the time of the

Prophet Muhammad and the first generation of Muslims, whereas Qur'anic Arabic projected a desert culture, one that preceded Robert by more than five centuries, one that was remote from him and also from his European contemporaries.

Robert could have produced a literal translation, and later scholars have faulted him for what seemed to be his loose, almost subjective rendition of the Qur'an, but this was not the case. Robert believed enough in the revelatory claims of the Qur'an to consult Muslims who had written commentaries. He consulted many such commentaries, including Tabari's, and while he never cited them by name, it is very clear that he used them, and preferred them to a literal rendering, especially with difficult passages.

Simply because *The Law of the Pseudo-Prophet Muhammad* is a paraphrase does not mean that it is a poor and misleading translation. Robert was trying to gauge what Muslims themselves took the Qur'an to mean. Robert understood what many of his European successors who attempted to translate the Qur'an did not understand: the long tradition of Arabic/ Muslim commentary could help non-Muslims in their effort to move between different languages, cultures and religions. Robert used Muslim Qur'an commentaries, whether through translation or by reference to them in Arabic, and he made his own 'loose' translations of difficult words or complex passages with knowledge gleaned from these same commentaries.

Some of his best efforts at engaged translation are the earlier, shorter Chapters. The shortest of all Qur'anic chapters is Chapter 108, 'Al-Kawthar.' Al-Kawthar itself is a rare word, often translated as 'abundance' or 'abundance of good', but Tabari, along with others, thought it referred to a river in Paradise, following a Tradition on the Night Journey and Ascent to Heaven, where Gabriel is said to have told the Prophet: 'What you see here is the spring of Kawthar. God Almighty has made you a gift of it.' Robert reflects the view of this tradition when he renders the verse:

> In the Name of God, Full of Compassion,
>> Ever Compassionate
>
> Surely we have prepared for you a fountain in Paradise.
> So pray to your Lord and sacrifice.
> For your enemy will surely lack helpers and progeny.
>> (108:1–3)

The general reference to 'abundance' becomes instead the specific mention of 'a fountain in Paradise'. Similarly, in the last line, the Qur'an simply refers to the enemy as 'cut off'. It does not allude to 'helpers and progeny', but another prominent medieval commentary – this one by Tabarsi, a twelfth-century Shi'ite scholar – does suggest that the enemy will have no children or progeny, and it seems likely that Robert used Tabarsi's insight to amplify his own translation.

A similar conclusion comes in considering the final Chapter, 114, 'Humankind', which asks for protection from the accursed one.

In the name of God Full of Compassion,
    Ever Compassionate

Repeat: I seek protection with the Lord of Creation
                        the King of Creation
                        the God of Creation

    From the malicious incantations
    Of the Accursed, whispering insinuations
    In the hearts of jinn and humankind both, fabrications.

Robert of Ketton uses the dreaded name of Satan, rather than the indirect appellation, in his own rendition of Chapter 114:

        Beseech the God of all things
        That He defend and free you
        From the Devil who penetrates human hearts...

Other instances of Robert's attention to Muslim commentaries and his interpolation or expansion of Qur'anic passages abound. Two from the later Medinan chapters underscore with special force his deep engagement with the text that he has decried as 'a book of lies'.

Chapter 22 is titled 'The Pilgrimage'. While it depicts, as one would expect, crucial elements of the *haj*, or canonical pilgrimage that takes place annually to Mecca, it begins with a reference to the 'earthquake of the Hour'.

> In the Name of God, Full of Compassion,
>> Ever Compassionate
>
> O people, keep your duty to your Lord;
> Surely the earthquake of the Hour is a portentous thing.

But 'the earthquake of the Hour' does not make sense by itself. It requires intertextual use of A Book of Signs to grasp its meaning. It becomes clear only when you read it with Chapter 99, 'The Earthquake'. There the Earthquake refers to the Final Day of Judgement, and Robert of Ketton has not only followed commentators but also made sense of the internal rhythms of Qur'anic logic when he introduces a paraphrase into his rendition of this verse:

> In the Name of God, Full of Compassion,
> Ever Compassionate
>
> Humankind, fear God,
> for the earthquake of the final hour
> on the Day of Judgement is to be feared.

Even while taking liberties with the Qur'anic text, he is making a general point ('fear God') into a specific caution: 'the earthquake of the final hour on the Day of Judgement' conjures the day already alluded to in the Opening Chapter, when God is depicted as not just the Source of Compassion, Ever Compassionate but also 'Master of the Day of

Determination or Judgement' (1:4). Robert gets the point right even though his translation exceeds the bounds set by some literal-minded critics.

Robert's sensitivity to Qur'anic language and its layered meaning is also apparent in his rendition of the latter part of Chapter 22, 'The Pilgrimage'. The crucial verse is 22:52. It has drawn the attention of almost all commentators, and also would-be translators, because it seems to refer to the concept of Lapse inherent in the Satanic Verses of 53:19:

> Have you then considered Lat and Uzza,
> And another, the third, Manat?
> Are the males for you and the females for Him?

The sequel of 53:20–25 erased the momentary doubt, if such existed, in the mind of Muhammad, but does 22:52 also refer to a hesitation or lapse in prophetic receivership? According to a literal translation, the answer is yes.

> Never sent we a messenger before you desiring anything
> but that Satan did not obstruct his desire.
> And God abolishes what Satan obstructs.
> Then does God establish His Signs. (22:52)

Yet lexical subtleties allow for another interpretation that sidesteps the inference of misguided prophecy:

> No messenger has been sent by God

> but that from his heart,
> influenced by devilish suggestions and delights,
> God wipes away the bad
> and ingrafts the good. (22:52)

If the first translation is more technically accurate, the second, from Robert, is more theologically adroit. Not only does he condense the phrases that have God abolishing what Satan obstructed before establishing His own Signs, but Robert also makes clear that the initial obstruction was *not* in the prophecy but rather in the reflex that preceded it. In other words, even while his heart could not expel Satan, the Prophet prior to his Prophecy is already blessed by Divine intervention: God intervenes, *before the delivery of prophecy*, to wipe away the bad and ingraft the good.

With ingenious translations such as these, Robert projects himself as peacefully disposed to the same enemy whom many of his co-religionists were intent on killing. Could it perhaps be that his outward antipathy for the Qur'an was a ruse against his enemies, a pose to deflect their animosity? In the atmosphere of the Crusades, and engaged by a patron (Peter the Venerable) already suspect for his irenic views, Robert had to be harsh on Muhammad; he had to denounce 'his book of lies'. Yet Robert's careful labour, his use of Muslim commentaries to understand what Muslims themselves believed to be the Qur'anic message, marked him as one with inward sympathy for Islam and for A Book of Signs.

The paradox of admiring your enemy is one not easily

grasped by those who have never translated. You may dislike someone or some idea, but still try to understand both the person and the concept that are alien to you. If it is Islam you dislike, and the Qur'an is the heart of Islam, then you have to resort to Muslims who believe in Muhammad's message in order to grasp what they 'mistakenly' think to be its truth. Though hostile to Islam, Robert was willing to trust Muslim scholars in trying to unravel what Muslims found believable in the 'false' prophecy of Muhammad. This was, after all, no ordinary book. It was a holy book, or so it claimed. As A Book of Signs, it was the lodestone of truth for the major spiritual and geopolitical rival of Christendom.

At the beginning of the twenty-first century, with religious Crusades still in evidence, Robert of Ketton's work points the way to other options for engaging Muslims. Translation can ennoble as well as belittle one's enemy. Since the Arabic Qur'an is intended to be the spiritual compass for humankind, its directives, even in English, hold out hope for all the children of Abraham – Jews and Christians as well as Muslims – and perhaps also for their cousins outside the fold of Abraham.

## CHAPTER 8

# Muhyiddin Ibn 'Arabi: Visionary Interpreter of Divine Names

## 1235 CE

A mystic philosopher, Muhammad Muhyiddin Ibn 'Arabi was also a bold interpreter of the Qur'an. He is renowned among those Muslim travellers on the mystical path known as Sufis. He inspired a new, deeply metaphorical approach to the Qur'an. He is known as Muhyiddin (the Reviver of Religion) because he sought to revive and transform Islamic spirituality. Many regard him as al-Shaykh al-Akbar (the Greatest Master) in the long and illustrious line of Sufi masters, those seekers of truth who also guide others on the journey towards the Unseen.

Ibn 'Arabi was born in Seville in 1165, when southern Spain was still under Muslim rule and at the axis of major religious, cultural and scientific exchanges. He travelled far from his European birthplace: after visiting many sites in North Africa and the Fertile Crescent, he settled down in Damascus, where he died in 1240 CE. He was not only a peripatetic but also a visionary with a prolific pen. He wrote more than 300 books, some quite short but others, including his *magnum opus*, *The Meccan Openings*, were enormous.

Ibn 'Arabi's works are at once compelling and inaccessible. He esteemed experience over knowledge. Clearly he expected his readership to have already internalized the Qur'an to such an extent that there would be no need for him to offer extended citations. He shared with others his own engagement with the One partially, elliptically. By its very nature such engagement can never be fully taught or adequately learned. It must be a private secret, shared only with the Prophet and with the Almighty, the Supreme Wisdom. But the channel for Wisdom is the Qur'an. It is the sole source for guidance. It is also the ultimate challenge. 'Everything comes from the Qur'an and its treasures,' declared the Greatest Master, Ibn 'Arabi, but then he added, 'Plunge into the ocean of the Qur'an if you can breathe deeply. Otherwise, content yourself with the study of commentaries on its apparent meaning.'

Ibn 'Arabi was a deep-sea diver in the ocean of the Qur'an. One of his most enduring works was *Fusus al-Hikam* or *Bezels of Wisdom*. Like bezels or cloves, each of the chapters must be peeled back, examined in the minutiae of Ibn 'Arabi's technical vocabulary and intricate style, in order to get at its kernel. When one makes this effort, one discovers the hidden key to prophecy, to the Qur'an, and to Islam. It comes through meditation on the figure of individual prophets – from the first man, Adam, who was also the first prophet, up to the perfect man and the final prophet, the Prophet Muhammad.

There are three steps to take on the path to truth. The first, indispensable step is sincerity. Every seeker must be pure in motive; a disposition of sincerity is the sine qua non of the quest for truth. Experts in every field, observed Ibn 'Arabi, set down technical terms unknown to others unless learned from them. Every group has a science. Logicians, grammarians, arithmeticians, astronomers, theologians, philosophers – each use technical terminology not familiar to the uninitiated. The exception is Sufism. Here the sincere seeker must enter among mystics, having no news of their technical terms. 'Then,' explains Ibn 'Arabi, 'God opens up the eye of his understanding. He takes from his Lord at the beginning of his tasting, even though he had no news of the terminology they were using. Little by little this sincere seeker understands everything they are talking about, as if he himself had established their technical terms. He finds it a self-evident knowledge, one that wells up from inside him and is part of his deepest identity.'

Sincerity leads to the second step, insight, as the Qur'an avows:

> Say: 'This is my way:
>> invite (men and women)
>> to God
>> with clear insight. (12:108)

Yet the invitation does not produce the same insight in each seeker. Just as sincerity is marked by degrees – not all are equally sincere, so all seekers do not have the same potential for knowledge or insight. Ibn 'Arabi explains the stages of insight with reference to one of his favourite Qur'anic passages:

> And we have given you
> Seven verses for repetition,
> And the Great Recitation. (15:87)

*The Meccan Openings* are an extended commentary on this verse. They were revealed to Ibn 'Arabi when he was on the pilgrimage to Mecca. Just as myriad insights derived from this single Qur'anic verse, so its truth was conveyed to Ibn 'Arabi in a single moment, through the apparition of a youth. The youth vanished before Ibn 'Arabi could meet him, but as he left he told Ibn 'Arabi: 'I am the Recitation (that is, the Qur'an), and the seven verses for repetition.' In other words, the youth claimed to be a divine emissary: 'I am the sum total of the Qur'anic revelation, characterized by seven repeated or doubled verses.' Like an earlier dream where Ibn 'Arabi saw himself united with the stars and with the letters of the Arabic alphabet, the youth personified for the mystic seer the sum total of meaning. He was the mediator of the (seven) doubled, whether they be the actual verses of the Qur'an or seven of the Divine Names or seven mystical states induced by those verses and names.

The seven verses to which the Qur'an itself is referring are likely to be the seven verses of the Opening Chapter of the Qur'an:

(1)  In the Name of God, Full of Compassion, Ever
     Compassionate

(2)  Praise to the Lord of all Creation,

(3)  Full of Compassion, Ever Compassionate,

(4)  Master of the Day of Determination,

(5)  You alone do we worship,
     From You alone do we seek alleviation

(6)  Guide us to the path of True Direction,

(7)  The path of those whom You favour,
     Not of those who cause You anger,
     Nor of those who took to the path of deviation. (1:1–7)

Ibn 'Arabi implies a parallel between *The Meccan Openings* given to him by the 'youth' and the Opening Chapter given by Gabriel to the Prophet Muhammad. Its three directives encode three stages or levels of sincerity. They are graded from lower to higher. The first or lowest is the sincerity of the masses. It requires sincerity in one's deeds and words ('You alone do we worship'). For the second or higher group, who are the elite, sincerity in deeds and words produces insight into the meaning of servitude and dependence ('From You alone do we seek alleviation'). Beyond the masses and the elite there is yet another group. They are the elite of the elite, not because of their social standing or their pious observance but because of their patience. The elite of the elite are sincere, like the masses, and insightful, like the elite, but they also persist and persist and persist. They embody patience, according to the Qur'anic dictum:

Persist with truth, persist with patience. (103:3)

Patience is the third step. It derives from sincerity and insight, yet offers its own special reward. For the elite of the elite, the outcome of sincerity, insight and patience is awareness of spiritual states. The patient seeker becomes receptive to the full experience of the Divine and so to the meaning of technical terms reserved for those who cry out: 'Guide us on the Straight Path'.

Sincerity, insight and patience take one to the threshold of Ibn 'Arabi's approach to Qur'anic truth. It discloses the notion of parallelism that pervades his approach to the Qur'an. Whatever seems to be a mere pairing or doubling, such as the two names of God – Full of Compassion, Ever Compassionate – or the two groups with whom God is angry or who have gone astray – such pairings are much more than a mere juxtaposition of similar words or themes. 'For every sign there is an outward and an inward, a limit and a potential,' according to a Tradition of the Prophet Muhammad. If the visible world is filled with signs, they remain mere signs, possible beacons of light but still dim or dark, until human creatures recognize their creatureliness as a potential to reflect the attribute of God as Creator. Another Tradition ascribed to the Prophet Muhammad echoes the familiar biblical phrase: 'God created man in His own image' (Genesis 1:27). In His own image means, for Ibn 'Arabi and many other mystics, the possibility of humans reflecting Divine traits but always within limits. Divine traits are not equivalent to the Divine essence, which remains unattainable and hidden. But Divine traits have been disclosed to humankind through the names of God, His Beautiful Names, and the names are portals to the Divine potential in each of us.

For Ibn 'Arabi, the Beautiful Names of God were more than epithets to be recited in prayer or to be invoked at times of distress. They were the outward signs of the inward mystery of the universe, the pairing of all created with all potential forms of existence. Muhammad was the exemplar of this pairing. He was the servant, mirroring the Lord so fully that He was the perfect man. He was a human torch reflecting the Divine Light. He offered in the defining moments of his life clues for all to understand. From the initial revelation to the flight to Medina to the farewell pilgrimage, the life of Muhammad provided signs for believers to ponder, grasp and apply to their own lives. But the foremost sign for the advanced seeker, the elite of the elite, is the Night Journey, the single night when Muhammad went from Mecca to Jerusalem to the Highest Heaven and back to Jerusalem and then to Mecca.

The Night Journey for Ibn 'Arabi represents the inner, spiritual journey that each seeker must pursue and experience for himself. It is a journey to God, into God and then from God. And so when the seeker sincerely yearns to gain clear insight into the form of God hidden within his own human form, 'God makes him journey through His Names,' explains Ibn 'Arabi, 'in order to cause him to see His Signs within him. Thus the servant comes to know that he is what is designated by every Divine Name – whether or not that Name is one of those described as "Beautiful".'

One of Ibn 'Arabi's most difficult yet most pivotal insights is that the Divine Names are themselves vehicles to understanding the Divine within us. They are labelled in the Qur'an as His *Beautiful* Names:

> For God's are the most Beautiful Names,
> so call Him by them. (7:180)

Yet not all the Divine Names are beautiful, at least by human standards. Some of the Divine Names are majestic or severe: God as the Punisher, as the Avenger, as the Exacter, as the One who commands death. Ibn 'Arabi does not flinch from seeing the full spectrum of Divine Names as the treasure given to the servant, with the human acknowledging God and submitting to Him. They are an invitation to return to one's origins, to know one's true self.

For Ibn 'Arabi, remembering the Divine Names is a collective homage to the Lord of all worlds. Ibn 'Arabi interprets the Qur'anic verse to mean: To God belong the Most Beautiful Names, and even though the essence of God is unknowable and invisible, the observable world – the planets and stars, the earth, and all of nature – can manifest those same Names; it can partake of the Divine Names as physical and tactile, visible and sentient. However, the Unseen only unfolds its mysteries, it only becomes manifest to human beings when individuals, recognizing the Names as the Most Beautiful

Names, make those nominal traits their own actual traits. This requires more than book knowledge or good behaviour. It comes through patience, persistent patience on the path. Patience yields experience of the Divine depth, an experience that shatters and transforms those humans, the best of humans, who strive to appropriate God's Names as their own.

How many names are there? God has innumerable Names, perhaps as many as 300. There are 300 saints, according to Ibn 'Arabi, and each of them corresponds to one of the 300 Divine traits. Yet even for the saints it is not the Names in themselves that are important, but rather the parallel between the holy person who invokes a Name and the subsequent experience of living that Name without residual attachment to one's own needs or desires.

Only the deeply sincere, those who have achieved insight and persisted with patience, become known as saints. While saints, like others, make the spiritual journey from mundane, ordinary existence, they journey *within* God as the Prophet Muhammad did.

To journey within God means, of course, that it is God who incites the seeker as well as guides him to the highest destiny. 'Thus when God makes the spiritual seeker, or saint, travel through His Most Beautiful Names to the other Names and ultimately to all the Divine Names,' explains Ibn 'Arabi, 'he comes to know the transformation of his states and the states of the whole world. And when he has completed his share of the journey through the Names and has come to know the Signs that the Names of God gave him during that journey, he retraces his steps. On his return, he continues to pass through the different sorts of worlds, taking from each world that aspect of himself which he had left there and reintegrating it in his self, until he arrives back on earth.'

Ibn 'Arabi was granted his own parallel to the Night Journey and Ascent of the Prophet Muhammad. His nocturnal vision also took him to the Lote Tree of the Limit (53:14; see p. 30), where he saw among other things the four rivers. They too exemplify the correspondence of visible to invisible, of this world to the next, which runs through all Divine revelation. According to a tradition, the Prophet Muhammad 'saw four rivers flowing forth from its roots, two were outer, natural rivers, and two others were inner, spiritual rivers'. Gabriel had pointed out to the Prophet that 'the two inner ones are in the Garden of Paradise, while the two outer ones are the Nile and the Euphrates'. But Ibn 'Arabi is told that on the Day of Judgement the two outer ones will also become rivers of Paradise, making four rivers (of milk, honey, water and wine) promised to believers in the Qur'an. The four rivers also correspond to the Scriptures revealed to humankind. Together the four rivers constitute one great river, which is the meta-text. The first and largest is the Qur'an, which is also the inner reality of Muhammad. The three other rivers or tributaries that flow from the great river, then return back to it, are the Torah, the Psalms and the Gospel. All of them are markers or paths for human guidance, and all paths at the deepest level are 'straight'. All require sincerity, produce insight, and reward patience. All lead back to God.

Ibn 'Arabi attained a visionary experience with levels of insight that few believers, even the most dedicated seekers, could grasp. He was a genius, and remains for many the seal of spiritual wisdom in Islam, the Greatest Master, whose practice was derived from the Qur'an and nourished through engagement with its multiple meanings.

## CHAPTER 9

# Jalal ad-din Rumi: Author of the Persian Qur'an

1270 CE

Jalal ad-din al-Rumi was born in early-thirteenth-century central Asia. The Mongols had conquered much of the continent, forcing Rumi's father, Baha ad-din, to resettle at Konya in present-day Turkey. Rumi followed in his father's footsteps, and became a famous religious scholar. Then in mid-life he encountered a wandering dervish. While he had had some prior contact with Sufi masters, the encounter with Shamsuddin Tabriz (Shams) changed his life, and compelled Rumi to seek verse rather than prose as the literary conduit of his inner turmoil. In addition to a huge collection of poetry dedicated to Shams, Rumi dictated the *Mathnawi-e Ma'nawi*. Known as the Persian Qur'an, the *Mathnawi* consists of about 27,000 couplets; it is the largest mystical poem ever produced by a Muslim scholar. As well as writing poetry, Rumi founded a mystical order, known in Europe and America as 'the Whirling Dervishes'. He himself is often called simply Mawlana, or Our Master.

Mawlana, 'Our Master', resembled his contemporary, ash-

Shaykh al-Akbar, the Greatest Master. Like Ibn 'Arabi, Rumi was a devout Muslim, steeped in knowledge of the Qur'an and the spectrum of traditions linked to the Prophet Muhammad. Both men were learned in a range of sciences, from grammar and rhetoric to logic and law to philosophy and theology. Both were motivated to seek truth beyond the external form of ritual and rules. Both became exemplars, guiding others on the path to the Unseen.

Yet Rumi was also utterly unlike Ibn 'Arabi. Though the quest defined them as fellow travellers, they followed different signposts. While Ibn 'Arabi sought the inner meaning of the Qur'an in universal forms, Rumi sought its display in everyday wonders. In the verse of Rumi, tailors and shoemakers, cooks and gardeners become as much his subjects as philosophers or theologians or poets. Inanimate as well as animate beings find ways to praise God:

> I have not created men and jinn
> except to worship Me. (51:56)

For Rumi this Qur'anic injunction means not only man and spirits but all creation is to worship the Creator. Hence the true meaning of the Opening Chapter is to be found in the prayer of the garden, in the changing of seasons:

> You alone do we worship (1:5a) *is in winter the prayer of the
>   garden,*

*In spring, it says,* And from You alone do we seek alleviation.
(1:5b)
You alone do we worship *means: I have come to Your door;*
*Open the portal of joy, do not keep me any longer distressed.*
And from You alone do we seek alleviation *means:*
*From the wealth of fruits I have become broken –*
*O Helper, watch me well.*

Whereas Ibn 'Arabi was awestruck by the tiers of meaning within A Book of Signs, Rumi was captivated by the
Divine magic that infuses the natural world, from plants to
planets and, above all, to the sun. For Rumi the person
Shams, whose name meant 'sun', became the sun. He radiated Divine Favour, even though his rays illumined not bliss
but pain. Shams seemed an unlikely companion: he lived on
the edges of society and had no material wealth; his 'riches'
consisted of his inner energy as a magical force. Outsiders,
including family members, were puzzled that Rumi abased
himself to someone who was in every external sense his infe-
rior. Yet so transformed was Rumi when he met the
vagabond Shams that much of his poetry, including the
*Mathnawi,* became an ode to the inspiration of a man who
was more than a man: Shams or Shamsuddin (the Sun of
Religion) Tabrizi was the guide, the master, and the source
for Rumi; he evoked all the prophets of the past. His sun
became the standard for measuring goodness and good
fortune:

> *O friend,*
> *You came to see the Sun rise,*
> *But instead you see us,*
> *Whirling like a confusion of atoms –*
>
> *Who could be so lucky?*

The joy of their meeting causes not just words of ecstasy but an overflow of human energy, a dance that transforms the reclusive scholar into the whirling dervish. In another poem Rumi exclaims:

> *The Sufi is dancing*
> *Like the shimmering rays of the sun,*
> *Dancing from dusk till dawn.*
> *They say*, this is the work of the devil (28:15)
> *Surely then, the Devil we dance with*
> *Is sweet and joyous,*
> *And himself an ecstatic dancer.*
>
> *A secret turns within my breast,*
> *And with its turning*
> The two worlds (1:1) *turn.*
>
> *I don't know head or feet,*
> *Up or down –*
> *All is lost*
> *In this awesome turning.*

'In this awesome turning': Rumi pushes the limits of language to express the inner tumult of love. The tumult is occasioned by the planetary sun/the Divine Sun/the mystical Sun of Tabriz. A range of homonyms sifts through Rumi's bedazzled mind, but the Qur'anic anchor endures. 'The work of the Devil' (28:15) is acknowledged even though his intent is transformed by the greater energy of the dance. And not just the Devil but both worlds are also turned upside down. For Rumi, 'the two worlds' (1:1), that is the visible and the invisible worlds, this world and the next, are both mirrored in the heart of the lover, and turn with his turning.

Rumi's passion spills into verse, into celebration of nature, into music and dance, into love of Shams. Yet there is a constant echo of another love – the love of women. It may echo Rumi's actual feeling for women he knew, but at the same time it is woman as an ideal form, the image of the Divine Beloved. It is carnal love as spiritual love, the human body as the metaphor of the Divine Other and the conduit to heavenly desire. It is from the Qur'an that Rumi takes his cue:

Made attractive to men is the love of desires – women (3:14)
*God has made her attractive, so how can men escape her?*

*Since He created Eve* so that Adam might find repose in her
(7:189)
*How can Adam cut himself off from her?*

*The Prophet, to whose speech the whole world was enslaved,*
*   Used to say: 'Speak to me, O 'A'ishah!'*

*Like water, you may outwardly dominate woman,*
*But inwardly you are dominated by her and seek her.*

*The Prophet said that women totally dominate men of*
*   intellect and possessors of hearts.*

While Qur'anic passages frame this section of the *Math-nawi*, it is the reference to 'A'ishah that links the Prophet with the rest of humankind who are beholden to women. Such domination by women, rather than a sign of weakness, is a mark of 'men of intellect' and 'possessors of hearts'. Neither phrase comes directly from the Qur'an, yet both echo its spirit: those in the highest ranks are praised both as ones who are given knowledge (58:11) and those whom God 'wrote' faith in their hearts (58:22).

Rumi himself called his *Mathnawi* the Qur'an in Persian. Like the Prophet, he did not write but dictated it, as in a trance or under a spell. He inherited this form of poetry from past Persian masters, including the tenth-century Firdausi, whose *Shahnameh* remained the prototype of all *mathnawis*. It is didactic poetry cast in narrative form. One story elides into another, sometimes biting and chiding, at other times exalting and soothing. In his *Mathnawi* Rumi constantly combines and recombines Qur'anic with quasi-Qur'anic motifs, at the same time that he evokes the Prophet Muhammad through traditions, such as the one just cited about 'A'ishah. Once when a companion qualified Rumi's depiction of the *Mathnawi*, explaining that it was a 'mere' *tafsir* or commentary on the Noble Qur'an, Rumi exclaimed:

> *'You dog!*
> *Why is it not [the Qur'an]?*
> *You ass!*
> *Why is it not [the Qur'an]?*

*Whatever contains the words of prophets and saints radiates the lights of Divine secrets. Divine speech pours out of their pure hearts; it flows down in streams from their tongues.'*

The *Mathnawi*, along with the *Diwan-i Shams* (Poems of Shams), are indeed inspired, often ecstatic writing. Yet Rumi also left more sober accounts of his spiritual quest. Collected as anecdotes by his disciples after his death, in these one gets a sense of Rumi's awareness that not all can pursue his path, not all can gaze at the sun. Yet even the more sober seekers can, and should, appreciate the limits of a literal approach to faith and knowledge.

To understand the Qur'an, one must recognize the signs that go beyond the printed word. Too many settle for one-dimensional reading, thinking and hearing of the Qur'an, just as ordinary folk look only at the literal meaning of the saints' words. '"We've heard all this talk many times before," they say. "We've had enough of such words." But,' counters Rumi, 'it is God who has plugged up their ears and

eyes and hearts so that they see the wrong colour. They perceive Joseph as a wolf. Their ears hear the wrong sound.
They hear wisdom as nonsense and raving. And their hearts,
having become repositories for temptations and vain imaginings, perceive falsely. Having been knotted up with
compounded imaginings, their hearts have frozen solid like
ice in winter.

> God has sealed
> their hearts and ears,
> and veiled their eyes.' (2:7)

Yet some of Rumi's toughest critics were proficient in the
Qur'an. Many of them had memorized it. They felt exalted by
their correctness and their proficiency. They expected to be
praised for their singleminded diligence, not berated as deaf
and dumb and blind reciters.

Rumi reminded them of an early Qur'an reciter, Ibn
Muqri. 'Ibn Muqri reads the Qur'an correctly,' notes
Mawlana. 'That is, he reads the form of the Qur'an correctly
but he hasn't a clue as to its meaning. The proof of this lies in
the fact that when he does come across a meaning he rejects
it. He reads without insight, blindly. But God's treasure
houses are many, and God's knowledge is vast. If a man
reads one Qur'an knowledgeably, why should he reject any
other Qur'an?'

Rumi speculates on why some pursue truth while others
don't. He finds the answer within A Book of Signs. 'There is

an infinity of words,' he observes, 'but they are revealed according to the capacity of the seeker.

> And whatever there is,
> Its storehouses are with Us;
> And We only distribute it
> in allotted measures. (15:21)

Wisdom is like the rain: at the source there is no end to it, but it comes down in accord with what is best, more or less according to season.'

Elsewhere Rumi cites, then explains the Quranic command:

> Say: 'Even if the ocean were ink
> For (writing) the words of my Lord,
> The ocean would be exhausted
> Before the words of my Lord were exhausted,
> Even if We were to add another ocean to it.' (18:109)

'Now for fifty drams of ink,' explains Rumi, 'one can write out the whole Qur'an. This is but a symbol of God's knowledge; it is not the whole of His knowledge. If a druggist put a pinch of medicine in a piece of paper, would you be so foolish as to say that the whole of the drugstore is in this paper? In the time of Moses, Jesus and others, the Qur'an existed; that is, God's Word existed; it simply wasn't in Arabic.'

At the same time, not all of God's words, either in Arabic

or any language, are of equal benefit. 'The best words,' explains Rumi, 'are those that are few and to the point.

> Say: 'He is God the One
>    God the Ceaseless,
>    Unbegetting and Birthless,
>    Like unto Him is no one.' (112)

Although these words from the Chapter of Sincerity are few in form, they are preferable to the lengthy Chapter of the Cow (2) by virtue of being to the point.'

Why is the Chapter of Sincerity considered so full of merit and grace, conferring blessing after blessing? Because the Prophet himself once said: 'The Chapter of Sincerity is equivalent to one third of the Qur'an.' In this sense, not just Rumi but many saints have observed that whoever recites the whole of the Qur'an should recite the Chapter of Sincerity three times at the end in keeping with the Prophetic saying that if you should miss some portion in your recitation, the three times that you recite the Chapter of Sincerity will be equivalent to having recited the entire Qur'an!

Rumi generated an appeal that has stood the test of time. At once epic narrative and metonymic verse, the *Mathnawi* or Persian Qur'an is the epitome of his greatness. Supplementing it are the poems to Shams, instructive tales and the order of Whirling Dervishes. Through these legacies he, more than any other mystical poet, has exerted a profound impact on generations of Muslims throughout Asia, from Samarkand to Sumatra. Devotees also celebrate his birthday in America and Europe. The annual Rumi Festival combines the same ecstatic elements of verse and dance initiated by the master:

> *Do not look for God.*
> *Look for one*
>   *Looking for God.*
> *But why look at all? –*
>   *He is not lost.*
>   *He is right here,*
>
> *Closer than your breath.*
>
> *I am filled with splendour,*
>   *Spinning with your love.*
>
> *It looks like I'm spinning around you,*
>   *But no – I'm spinning around myself!*

Can one monitor the sincerity of those who invoke the author of the Persian Qur'an? Because Mawlana now spins around himself as much in North America as in Anatolia, because he is as popular in the Carolinas as in Konya, he has become the currency not just for Sufi seekers but also for spiritual merchants. Deepak Chopra, Demi Moore and even Madonna have claimed to connect with the Whirling Dervish. In the twenty-first century Mawlana has indeed become a symbol for celebrities but whether this ubiquity taints or devalues his original messages is for each reader, and also each believer, to decide.

# Asian Echoes

## CHAPTER 10

# Taj Mahal: Gateway to the Qur'anic Vision of Paradise

1636 CE

A Mughal monument in marble relates to A Book of Signs through the portal of death.

When Arjumand Banu Begam left this world, she took with her the light from the Shadow of God, the King of the World, the Ruler of Hindustan, her husband, Shah Jahan. Arjumand Banu is also known as Mumtaz Mahal, because in the eyes of her husband she was just that: *mumtaz mahal*, 'the choice of the realm'.

The future Emperor had first met her at the Mughal court in Agra. She had come at the invitation of her grandfather, the chief minister to his father, the Emperor Jahangir. The young prince was smitten with her limpid beauty. They were betrothed in 1607, and then married in 1612. Though he had two other wives, he had but one daughter by another wife. Mumtaz Mahal produced fourteen children, of whom only seven survived, but four were sons and one was destined to become his father's successor, the Emperor Awrangzeb.

Mumtaz Mahal had died in 1631 giving birth to their fourteenth child. Away on a military campaign, Shah Jahan had not been at her side. Twenty-five years of bliss had vanished, replaced by grief, a hollow in his heart. Intent on honouring in death the woman who had been the centre of his life, he vowed to build her a monument that would be a visible, majestic prayer imploring the Almighty to join his soul with hers, until the Day of Judgement.

No expense was spared to construct this monument. Begun in 1632, the Taj Mahal was set in a complex of fountains and trees, gates and mosques, walks and walls that crisscrossed forty-two acres on the bank of the Jumna River near the Red Fort guarding the capital city of Agra. It was finished in 1636. For such an intricate monument four years of construction was astonishingly brief. Vast marble blocks had to be quarried, then shaped, the intricate inlay work commissioned, huge gateways and magnificent access routes provided. There were also calligraphic inscriptions. A few were in Persian, but most were in Arabic and drawn from the Noble Qur'an.

For the Emperor, the meaning of the Taj Mahal is inseparable from A Book of Signs; its passages define each and every entrance to the tomb. There are more extensive Qur'anic citations in the Taj Mahal than in any other Muslim tomb complex. Though most visitors never read these verses, they embody the message of the grieving Emperor.

The tomb of the deceased queen stands at the end of an exquisite garden. The garden is like other Persian and Indian tomb gardens. It suggests a celestial garden of pleasure, and projects the grand design of the Almighty in the world above. Yet only in the Taj Mahal do we find heaven mirrored on earth with words as well as images that flow from the Noble Qur'an. The Taj Mahal replicates heaven but not any heaven; it is a Muslim heaven, modelled on the imagination of Ibn 'Arabi.

Ibn 'Arabi never travelled beyond North Africa, Syria and Arabia, yet his fame resonated throughout Asia. Though Muslim seekers of truth were divided, then as now, about the merit of his teachings, his vision of heaven was never subject to dispute. Heaven was seen as a grand and radiant space. Its centrepiece was the divine throne, borne up by four angels. It is the desire of every earthbound form to ascend, to mirror that highest wonder of symmetrical power, the Divine throne, and the Taj Mahal fulfils that desire. It both crowns the space in which it is located and, as a perfect square, each of its corners marked by a minaret, it mirrors the highest abode, the throne of the Almighty.

Perfection, for Ibn 'Arabi, was never singular or one-dimensional. It always had to be layered, the outside and the inside refracting different tangents of the same divine source. The tomb refracts the power of the Divine gaze both outwardly to those who see it as they approach but also inwardly to those who gaze out from behind the marble filigree windows.

The Qur'anic vision that informs the Taj Mahal is announced at the outset. As one enters through the south arch gateway, it is Chapter 89, the Dawn or Daybreak, that sets the tone for what lies ahead. At the conclusion of its otherworldly vista the Lord of Life announces:

> O soul in repose,
> return to your Lord,
> pleased and accepted.
> Join the company of My servants,
> Enter into My Garden. (89:27–30)

Expanding the same theme in the north arch gateway is a band of three shorter but contiguous Chapters: Chapter 93, 'The Morning Light', Chapter 94, 'The Expansion', and Chapter 95, 'The Fig'. All echo the hope of the world to come but perhaps none so vividly as the first, the Chapter of the Morning Light:

In the Name of God, Full of Compassion, Ever Compassionate

> By the morning light
> And by the darkening night
> Your Lord has not forsaken you –
> there is no slight.
>
> The Hereafter is far better for you
> than this (first) life.
> Your Lord will lavish [bounties] upon you,
> and you will know delight.

Did he not find you an orphan,
then give you respite?
Find you unaware,
then guide you aright?
Find you wanting,
and then provide?

So as for the orphan, do not oppress,
So as for the supplicant, do not suppress,
And as for the bounties of your Lord, proclaim them.
(93)

'Night' in the second line may be a metaphor referring to the long period when the Prophet Muhammad had not received revelation prior to the disclosure of this Chapter. Now the morning brings with it a further revelation and also a hope: that the hereafter will be better than this life. This is because the Lord will lavish His bounties upon Muhammad and, by extension, on all who accept his prophecy. Together they will know delight without end. It is as if the Qur'anic verse is the foretaste of that delight that will be known to all believers in the world to come.

Not only the north/south gateways but also the tomb as well as the cenotaph of Mumtaz Mahal – all are adorned by Qur'anic verses. In each case the verses have been carefully selected; they fit together as seamlessly as the pieces of marble that have inlaid flowers or geometric designs etched on their surfaces. They are among the most familiar verses from the

Qur'an, evoking the glories of Paradise time and again.

On the tomb itself one finds beauty enfolding beauty, the sense of the verses matching the ethereal white of the marble and soft pastels and forms of the floral inlays. The arches to the tomb are connected by a continuous expression of Chapter 36, 'Ya Sin'. Often 'Ya Sin' is called the heart of the Qur'an. It is recited in full when someone's dying. As if to emphasize the liturgical practice in stone, the verses of 'Ya Sin' mark the north arch, since in the cosmology of heaven it is to the north that the departing soul leaves this world to meet the Lord of Life. These are some of the verses from 'Ya Sin' that look down from their marble perch:

> A Sign for them is the earth when dead;
> We revive it, and produce grain from it,
> Of which they partake.
>
> And We have put orchards
> Of dates and grapes thereon,
> And caused springs to flow on it,
>
> That they may eat of its fruit,
> Though they did not make it themselves;
> So will they not be grateful?
>
> Glory to the One who created mates,
> All of them from what the earth produces,
> And what they don't know.

And a Sign for them is the night;
We end the day with it, and lo –
They are steeped in darkness.

And the sun runs its course,
That is determined by the Almighty,
The Omniscient;

And for the moon
We have determined phases,
Until it returns to a tiny crescent.

The sun is not to overtake the moon,
And the night does not outstrip the day,
As each travels in its own orbit…

So glory to the One who holds
Sovereignty over all things,
And to whom you will be returned. (36:33–40, 83)

Each of the doors set within these massive arches is also marked by a full Qur'anic chapter on the external gates: Chapter 81 'The Rolling Up', on the south; Chapter 82 'The Splitting', on the west; Chapter 84, 'The Bursting Open' on the north; and Chapter 98, 'The Evidence', on the east. All promise the cataclysmic end of life's pleasure and pain.

The display of the Qur'an is then replicated on the interior part of these same tomb gates, with three full Chapters: Chapter 67, 'The Dominion', Chapter 48, 'The Victory' and

Chapter 76 'The Human Being' as well as the fragment from another: Chapter 39, 'The Crowds'. This last expresses the need to both acknowledge God's mercy and submit to His will:

> Say: 'O my servants
>> Who have transgressed against their own souls!
>> Do not despair
>> Of God's mercy,
>> For God forgives all sins!
>> Indeed, God is the epitome
>> Of forgiveness and mercy!
>>
>> And turn to your Lord
>> And submit to Him
>> Before the torment comes upon you,
>> After which you will not be helped. (39:53–4)

Qur'anic script, scrolled across the gates, the arches and the tomb doors of the Taj Mahal, extends to the cenotaphs. Unusual if not unprecedented in Islamic art are the double cenotaphs marking the resting place of Mumtaz Mahal. One is the dummy upper cenotaph. The other is the real, lower cenotaph. Both display a profusion of signs from the Noble Qur'an but perhaps none is so evocative as the reciprocal and symmetric citations found on the lower cenotaph. They consist of the ninety-nine Beautiful Names of God. The three most common of the beautiful names are given in an inscription on the north end of the cenotaph:

> He is God, there is no god but He.
>
> He knows the unseen and the seen.
>
> He is Full of Compassion, Ever Compassionate. (59:22)

And then the other ninety-six Beautiful Names are divided into six rows of sixteen each on the west and the east side of the cenotaph. Each name etches the qualities of the Divine that have inspired Muslims through the ages, from Ibn 'Arabi to his Asian successors who crafted the Taj Mahal as the model of heaven.

Imprisoned in late life by his son, the Emperor Awrangzeb, who feared being denied the throne, Shah Jahan spent his last seven years gazing at the Taj Mahal from across the Jumna River. Did the grieving, dethroned Emperor remember, and recite, the Beautiful Names that linked him both to the Divine Beloved and to his earthly beloved? Did he wish to be buried next to Mumtaz Mahal? It seems so, for his was a very quiet, almost secret burial. There was no state funeral, no public ceremony, not even a proper Islamic funeral. Instead, we are told, 'a few of the eunuchs and others, contrary to the custom of illustrious kings and the practice of his ancestors, placed his coffin early in the morning on a boat and carried it by way of the Jumna river to the Taj Mahal, which he had erected for this purpose.' In death as in life he shared the same space with the one who, for him, epitomized the beauty of this world, just as his monument to her radiated the splendour of the next.

## CHAPTER 11

# Ahmad Khan: Indian Educator and Qur'an Commentator

## 1884 CE

How can science be reconciled with religion? Believers from every major religious tradition have tried to answer this question since science became the key to technological progress, economic success and, most importantly, political/military dominance. It is impossible to imagine the emergence of Western Europe, North America or more recently Japan without crediting the instrumental power of modern science.

The Judaeo-Christian world pegged the problem of science to the work of Charles Darwin, and especially to his concept of evolution. Instead of an active agent shaping the world and humankind, Darwin offered an innate law of nature that was neither an intelligent first cause nor an interventionist benign creator. Instead he posited a long-term evolutionary process to explain both the continuity and change observable in the world of phenomena.

The Islamic world faced the crisis of modern science not through Darwinian logic but through European presence: by the nineteenth century, France, England and the Netherlands had become major powers in parts of Africa and Asia with Muslim majorities. And among Muslim elites subjected to British rule in Northern India none was more renowned, or more reviled, than Sir Sayyid Ahmad Khan (1817–98). Sir Sayyid, as he was most often known, since he was both descended from the Prophet Muhammad's family and honoured with a knighthood by the Queen of England, gained widespread fame as the foremost public intellectual of pre-Partition India. His energy was prodigious, his activities numerous and his achievements astonishing. He formed a scientific society for the translation of European scientific writings into Urdu, the literary language for most North Indian Muslims at the time. He also founded a major university, Aligarh Muslim University, for Muslim elites, and it became the benchmark for vilifying as well as praising him. It was modern precisely because its faculty, many of them initially Europeans, used English – not Urdu or Arabic or Persian, the Muslim languages for North India – to teach the range of subjects deemed important for science.

Sir Sayyid was engaged by science, but also mindful of the demands of religion. He saw that British administration of India abetted, even if it did not directly support, Christian missionary activities aimed at all groups, but especially at Muslims. European scientific researchers also challenged Islam. Known as Orientalists because they studied Islamic texts from the Orient, they learned Arabic and Persian (and occasionally Urdu) not to become Muslims but to assess the accuracy of Muslim claims about the sources of their belief and ritual, their law and practice. Caught between missionary polemicists and academic Orientalists, Sir Sayyid sought a middle way: to stress the sources as essential, the Qur'an above all. The Bible was also deemed important, and Sir Sayyid produced a unique, if partial, commentary on the Gospels (*Tabyin al-Kalam*, 1862).

In later years, however, Sir Sayyid turned his attention to a new, and scientific, study of the Qur'an (1880–95). He laid out principles for his modern commentary, and used them as a signpost for the future that was also a buffer against the past. He critiqued the traditional commentators, such as Tabari, Razi and Zamakhshari. They were preoccupied, in his view, with secondary problems. While they framed the Qur'an with reference to law or theology, and defended its eloquence against poetry and other works of rhetorical excellence, these were not issues of critical import in the modern age. What was paramount now was attention to foundational principles. It was these that had to be clarified, then applied to the range of evidence in the Qur'an.

For Sir Sayyid there were fifteen basic principles. They informed his commentary, and he argued, by extension, that they should inform all future commentaries.

1. God is all Powerful and all Prescient; He alone is the Creator of all that is.
2. God has sent prophets, including Muhammad, to guide humankind.
3. The Qur'an is the authentic revelation of God's eternal Word.

4. The Qur'an was revealed to Muhammad by Divine inspiration (with or without an angelic intermediary like Gabriel).

5. Nothing in the Qur'an could be wrong or incorrect or ahistorical.

6. The Divine attributes exist only in their essence.

7. The Divine attributes are identical with God's Self and are also eternal.

8. Though the attributes have no limits, God created the laws of nature and through them channelled His Wisdom and His Power.

9. Nothing in the Qur'an can be contrary to the laws of nature.

10. The present text of the Qur'an is at once complete and final.

11. Every Chapter and every verse in every Chapter follow a chronological order.

12. There is no such thing as abrogation (*naskh*), using a later text to trump an earlier one with which it seems to disagree.

13. The revelatory process of the Qur'an developed in stages.

14. Major teachings of the Qur'an – the End of Time, the Realm of Angels, the Role of Demons, and the Structure of the Universe – cannot be contrary to the laws of nature, or the teachings of modern science; they must be interpreted in light of these 'recent' truths.

15. Both the direct and indirect expressions in Qur'anic language point to the possibilities of development in human

society, and must be studied for their relevance to contemporary social life.

On the basis of these fifteen principles Sir Sayyid divided
all Qur'anic verses into two categories. It was not the clear or
ambiguous dyad known to Tabari and also Ja'far as-Sadiq.
Instead, Sir Sayyid framed verses as either essential or symbolic. The essential offered the irreducible core of faith, while
the symbolic were open to multiple interpretations, allowing
the believer to explain ages and circumstances far removed
from those of the Prophet Muhammad in early-seventh-cen-
tury Arabia.

If Sir Sayyid distanced himself from classical commentators, he also alienated their contemporary successors, the
'ulama, or learned scholars. They openly opposed him, especially after he began to publish his Qur'an commentary
serially, making each section available to an expanded
reading public. Through the printed press, Sir Sayyid dis-
seminated blistering attacks on his critics. The standard
commentaries on the Qur'an and the six classical collections
of Hadith withered under the lens of his rationalist review.
Many of those commentaries were demonstrable fabrications,
in his view, but even more, they were based on the reliability
of individuals rather than a logical critique of the text itself.
Sir Sayyid did not accept collections of Hadith as a basis for
true religion. At most, he argued, they could offer a historical
reflection on the ideas and attitudes of the first generations of
Muslims. (On this point, as on others, his view elided with

those of European scientizers, the textual Orientalists.)

In all his endeavours Sir Sayyid was trying to demythologize and to rationalize A Book of Signs. Miracles have no place in his approach to the Qur'an. The account of Muhammad's Night Journey and His Conversation at the Lote Tree of the Limit, for instance, are not to be taken at face value. They are neither physical nor spiritual experiences, but a dream. Sir Sayyid posited that no man, even a prophet, can have a direct vision of God. What mystics depict is due to their spiritual intensity not to supernatural powers or the interruption of nature.

A graphic example of Sir Sayyid's militantly rationalist approach to the Qur'an comes in his view of the Chapter entitled 'Muhammad'. The key phrase is:

> Set them free, whether as a favour or through ransom.

The phrase occurs in a passage that refers to the disposition of unbelievers whom the Muslims have fought (and defeated):

> So when you meet in battle those who disbelieve,
> smite their necks;
> Then when you have overcome them,
> make them prisoners
> but afterwards set them free,
> whether as a favour or through ransom,
> so that the toils of war may be ended. (47:4)

For Sir Sayyid this verse amounts not just to a limit on the treatment of prisoners of war but to a categorical denial of all slavery. Implicit in this revelation is a call for the liberation of slaves. Because the verse occurred near the end of the Prophet's lifetime, when he had just re-entered Mecca in the famous peace pilgrimage, Sir Sayyid called it the *Ayah hurriya* (the verse of liberation). He regarded its message as applicable for all Muslims in all periods. That it was not always observed, he viewed as not the fault of the Qur'an but of previous generations of Muslims – or unenlightened readers of his own generation. They had failed to grasp the revelatory import of the Qur'an.

Similarly, with reference to the age-old question of polygamy, Sir Sayyid did not accede to either the missionary onslaught or the Orientalist critique of Muslim practice. Instead, he showed that the key element for a valid Muslim interpretation, at once rationalist and modernist, lay in the opening verses of the Chapter on Women:

> And if you fear you cannot
> Do justice by the orphans,
> Then marry women who please you,
> Two, three, or four;
> But if you fear you won't be equitable,
> Then one, or a legitimate bondmaid of yours.
> That way it is easier for you not to go wrong. (4:3)

Emphasizing the phrase 'if you fear you won't be equitable', he argues that the basis for Muslim marriage is not love but justice. Since a man cannot treat more than one woman equitably, polygamy is inherently impossible and unIslamic. Devout Muslims, in marriage as in ownership, must always strive to be just. The age-old custom of polygamy, still practised in many Muslim societies, was deemed to be a case of mistaken interpretation at best, wilful neglect of principle at worst.

Whether interpreting the Qur'an to oppose slavery or to show the limits on polygamy, Sir Sayyid argued time and again that the work of God can never be in conflict with the word of God. Since nature and its laws are divinely sanctioned, A Book of Signs will always undergird the principle and practice of science.

And the scientific principle extends to religion. During a speech that he gave in Lahore, in the Padshahi Mosque built by the Emperor Shah Jahan, Sir Sayyid called for a new science of religious talk or theology ('ilm al-kalam). 'We need a new science of theology,' he urged, 'by which we should either refute the doctrines of modern science or show how they are in conformity with the articles of Islamic faith.'

For Sir Sayyid, the question had a clear answer: science was unveiling the new face of God for Muslims as well as non-Muslims. The only way forward for scholars of Islam was to show how the articles of Islamic faith conform to God's Wisdom and Power in every age of humankind.

## CHAPTER 12

# Muhammad Iqbal: Pakistani Poet Inspired by Qur'anic Motifs

## 1935 CE

Poets achieve fame not just in their lifetime but across generations. For many Muslims, especially those of India and Pakistan,
who seek a contemporary counterpart to Rumi, the most obvious candidate would be Muhammad Iqbal (1873–1938). A
Kashmiri, a Punjabi, an Indian, a Pakistani by adoption, Iqbal
combined competing identities, but above all he was a visionary
poet whose vision was framed by the Qur'an.

Iqbal was born into a devout Muslim family in 1873. His
ancestors were Hindus from Kashmir. Though Brahmins,
they had converted to Islam during the reign of Shah Jahan.
Iqbal's family later moved from the Kashmir valley to the
plains of the Punjab, where he received a thorough education
that was both religious and secular. He loved Arabic for the
great works of literature and philosophy that it opened up to
him, but above all for the resonance of the Qur'an. He wrote
poetry from an early age. It took him into another realm,
the realm of the imagination, helping him to engage with the
change of fortune that confronted him and his fellow

Muslims. By the turn of the new century the worldly fates of Indian Muslims had become very sad. Mughal glory had been superseded by British rule.

In 1905 Iqbal went to England, obtaining his law degree at Cambridge University. He also continued to study literature and, at the behest of one of his English professors specializing in Persian literature, he later went to Germany. In Munich he earned his doctorate, before returning to India at the age of thirty-five. Though he practised law for a living, it was poetry that animated him. It gave meaning to his life, and earned him high renown.

At first he wrote verse in Urdu, but then switched to Persian, while still writing some lyrics in Urdu. In both languages he tried to merge the modern world with the Muslim aesthetic tradition, weaving new ideas into the many, many poems he composed.

In his poetry Iqbal exhorted people, particularly the young, to stand up and face life's challenges boldly. The central theme and main source of his message was the Qur'an. He considered the Qur'an to be much more than a book of religion or scripture: it was for him a source of foundational principles upon which to build a coherent system of life. The result was Islam. If Islam were based on the permanent, absolute values given in the Qur'an, reasoned Iqbal, it would bolster collective and individual, public and private identity. It would undergird perfect harmony, balance and stability in the public sphere at the same time that it provided freedom of choice and equal opportunity for individuals in the private sphere. Everyone could, and should, develop his or her life within the guidelines of the Qur'an. The Qur'anic way eschewed both rank individualism and collective tyranny. It ruled out a private subjective relationship with God that accented personal salvation, but equally it debarred theocracy, rule in the name of God, and dictatorship, rule through brute power. Tyranny, whether religious or secular, countermanded the free spirit of Islam announced and promoted in the Qur'an.

Because Iqbal was a poet-philosopher, his goal was to marry dialogue to dialectics in a way that neither the Greeks nor their modern successors had done. In the Qur'an Iqbal found the model for a dialogue between God and man. It was continuous and multivalent. It began with man's complaint. In 1909, after returning from Europe to India, Iqbal chanted 'The Complaint' before a gathering of fellow Muslims. His soft voice and gentle rhymes belied the stark message: modern Muslims do have a complaint against God. It is a legitimate complaint framed by the trust of centuries, stretching back to the time of the Prophet. It is put at risk now, bemoaned Iqbal, by the despair of present-day circumstances:

> *We [Muslims] blotted out the smear of falsehood from the pages of*
> > *history*
> *We freed mankind from the chains of slavery.*
> *The floors of Your Ka'bah with our foreheads we swept,*
> *The Qur'an You sent us we clasped to our breast, [but now]*

*Your blessings are showered on homes of unbelievers, strangers all.*
*Only on the poor Muslim does Your wrath like lightning fall.*

It was not Iqbal's intent to reject God, or belief in God, with this lament, but many of the religious people of his time saw it differently. They accused him of taking liberties in addressing God so frankly. His manner, they groused, was more that of a drunken Sufi, like Rumi, than that of a sober scholar, like Tabari.

Iqbal pondered these responses. He also imagined what might be the response of God to his complaint. Four years later, in 1913, in his home city of Lahore, at the mosque built by the Mughal Emperor Shah Jahan – the same mosque where Sir Sayyid Ahmad Khan had spoken less than two decades earlier – Iqbal delivered God's answer to the complaint:

> *'All you drink the wine of bodily indulgence,*
> *Leading lives of ease without strife.*
> *Dare you call yourselves Muslims?*
> *What kinship of the soul can there be*
> *Between your ancestors and you?*
> *As Muslims your forefathers were honoured and respected;*
> *But you gave up the Qur'an and now by the world are rejected.'*

The human–Divine dialogue did not come easily to Iqbal. It burned his soul. Raw and stark, it imitated the arduous quest of Sufi masters from the Islamic past. Yet he challenged the present age to produce its own spiritual risk-takers, those who would dare to intercede on behalf of others, seeking God's blessing and pursuing knowledge of His Will. To this ancient dialogic form, familiar if not always acceptable to all Muslims, Iqbal brought a new content. His quest was to bridge Islam and the modern world without supporting colonialism or embracing atheism. As he said in another poem, echoing one of his favourite Qur'anic themes, Abraham in the fire (21:68–9):

> I broke the spell of modern learning
> I took away the bait and broke the trap.
> God knows with what indifference,
> Like Abraham, I sat in its fire!

As the fire of nationalism swept through India, stirring Muslims as well as Hindus and Sikhs, Iqbal tried to provide the answer to Abraham's dilemma. He eventually provided the answer not in verse but in prose. In 1928 he gave six lectures to Muslim students in Madras that were then published in a book entitled *Reconstruction of Religious Life in Islam*. In it Iqbal unfolds the Muslim past in the dialogic space of the European present. With the Qur'an as his litmus test, he critiques his intellectual ancestors. 'While Greek philosophy very much broadened the outlook of Muslim thinkers,' he laments, 'it on the whole obscured their vision of the Qur'an.' Yet the greatest of modern European thinkers, trying to wed science with progress, have also lost their way in the cosmos.

'Modern man, that is, modern European man,' observes Iqbal, 'has ceased to live soulfully, i.e. from within.'

To reconstruct religious life in Islam one must first relocate, grasp and celebrate life from within, the experience of the Other as a dimension of everyday life. Iqbal uses both the Qur'an in Arabic, A Book of Signs, and the Qur'an in Persian, Rumi's *Mathnawi*, to frame the arguments of *Reconstruction of Religious Life in Islam*. His goal is to find Muslim sources which can counter the challenge posed by European thinkers as well as colonial overlords. The Noble Qur'an and Mawlana's *Mathnawi* are the riposte to European luminaries, from Charles Darwin and Sigmund Freud to Bertrand Russell and Albert Einstein. 'With the reawakening of Islam,' writes Iqbal, 'it is necessary to examine, in an independent spirit, what Europe has thought and how far the conclusions reached by her can help us in the revision and, if necessary, reconstruction, of theological thought in Islam.' Because European social initiatives and technical achievements have benefited all humankind, one must apply a pragmatic test *even* to divine revelation. To the extent that the Qur'an confirms for modern man the eternal value of Gabriel's message to the Prophet Muhammad, it is because 'the general empirical attitude of the Qur'an engendered in its followers a feeling of reverence for the actual and ultimately made them the founders of modern science'.

Even as he was delivering these lectures in 1928, Iqbal seemed to recognize that he had let the jinn (or, as English speakers would say, the genie) out of the bottle. Though never citing Sir Sayyid Ahmad Khan by name, Iqbal was confirming that a new science of religion had to have an empirical strategy that conformed to modern science. As a result, however, the trust of God to humankind was no longer a book apart from other books; it was a book that stood tested, and confirmed, on the anvil of modern science, with its rules of evidence, its guidelines and its protocols. At the same time, science was divinized: embraced as the handmaiden of God, its rules were deemed to be His rules, its world His world. For the modern Muslim, as for their ancestors, the challenge was the same: never cease dialoguing with God. The question raised by modern science was the same question raised in every age: whose authority is it that makes and shapes the world?

'Whose world is this – yours or mine?' was how Iqbal formulated the query in one of his most haunting poems published in 1935, just three years before his death. 'The Wing of Gabriel' compressed meaning into sound, and made of the sound an echo that lingers. It was as though Iqbal the philosopher could only come to terms with the tragic separation of humanity from its divine source through verse:

### Whose World is This – Yours or Mine?

> On the morning of eternity Satan dared to say 'No',
> But how would I know why?
> Is Satan Your confidant, or mine?

*Muhammad is Yours.*
*Gabriel is Yours,*
*The Qur'an is Yours –*

*But this discourse,*
*This exposition in melodious tunes,*
*Is it Yours or is it mine?*

*Your world is illuminated*
*By the radiance of the star of Adam –*
*But whose loss was the fall of Adam, that creature of earth,*
*Was it Yours or was it mine?*

The key word of this poem is loss. The loss is occasioned by Adam's fall, so graphically told in the Qur'an:

And when We told the angels
to bow to Adam,
they bowed, except Iblis
– the One Who Despaired;
he refused, showing arrogance;
and he was a scoffer.

And We said, 'Adam,
dwell in the garden,
you and your wife,
and eat from it comfortably,
when and as you want.
But do not approach this particular tree,

lest you become wrongdoers.'

Then Satan made the two slip there,
and caused them to depart
the state they were in.
And We said, 'Descend in mutual antipathy,
yet you will have an abode
and belongings on earth for a while.'

Then Adam learned words from his Lord,
Who forgave him; for God is Forgiving,
Merciful. (2:34–7)

The Qur'anic accent on Adam's fate in the final couplet spins the whole poem into a different realm of possible meaning:

> *But whose loss was the fall of Adam, that creature of earth,*
> *Was it Yours or was it mine?*

Adam's moral failure on earth, Iqbal suggests, mirrored even as it presaged the fall of Muslims from public power in India. And God as well as humankind experienced the double loss, since the fall of Adam from heaven was also an epic moment of loss for the angelic realm. Just as the splendour of Paradise was reduced when Adam ceased to be part of the chorus echoing God's eternal praise, so the 'star of Adam' will illumine God's world less brightly when Indian Muslims are no longer at the forefront of the *ummah*, or global Muslim community.

It is a bold analogy to the Qur'an and to history. It is perhaps the major contribution of Muhammad Iqbal, the poet-philosopher, for his own generation, and for future generations, of believers: to underscore how the fates of humankind and the divine are inextricably intertwined. God has a stake in what happens below, just as the believer holds out hope for eternal bliss. The needs of the Lord and the servant are reciprocal. Neither is complete without the other. It is a cosmic tug-of-war that eludes the clunky prose of a theologian or the diatribes of a preacher. Only a poet-philosopher can voice it in poignant verse: *Whose world is this – Yours or mine?* The answer: both.

# Global Accents

## CHAPTER 13

# W. D. Mohammed:
# Qur'an as Guide to
# Racial Equality

## 1978 CE

To be black and Muslim in the United States of America has always been a challenge. It is a particular challenge for Imam W. D. Mohammed, the foremost spokesperson for more than two million African American Muslims. Since 1932, his father Elijah Muhammad had led the Nation of Islam. During the forty years that followed, the Nation of Islam had become known not only for its embrace of Islam but also for its racial separatism. W. D. Mohammed changed that attitude. In 1976 he became the leader and changed the group's name to the World-Community of al-Islam in the West, then to the Muslim American Society, and most recently to The Mosque Cares. In each phase W. D. Mohammed has championed Islam as an authentic American religion, and he has consistently opposed racism in all its expressions, especially among Muslims.

When W. D. Mohammed succeeded his father, his authority had been rejected by rivals, chief among them Minister Louis Farrakhan. In 1978 Minister Farrakhan revived the Nation of Islam with the same racial separatist message as

Elijah Muhammad. Quietly W. D. Mohammed has persisted in distancing himself from both his father and Farrakhan. To distinguish true Islam from false versions of Islam, he often refers to Islam as al-Islam, that is, *the* Islam – the real Islam – not its distortion in the old and new forms of the Nation of Islam.

In a 1978 speech entitled 'America: The Beautiful and the Beast', he demonstrated how thoroughly his view of Islam was grounded in a distinctive reading of the Qur'an. Imam W. D. Mohammed eschews racism. In its stead, he offers hope that Qur'anic precedents can inform the thinking of Caucasians as well as African Americans, non-Muslims along with Muslims, to make America the beautiful and not the beast.

> *God is a merciful God. All praises are due to Allah.*
>
> *Dear beloved people, the Holy Quran tells us to look at color. Not only that, the Holy Quran says that in the heavens and in the earth, and the workings between heaven and earth, as well as in yourselves too, that you will find instructing signs from God. God teaches us through His creation, He designed His creation to speak wisdom to the mind of the thinking man.*
>
> *How do you think that the Caucasian has come to the high position that he has in science and in other fields of human endeavors and achievements? It's because he got the message from the Quran and was able to see the problem in the Bible, separate his intelligence from the Bible and give his intelligence to the great kinds of*

*influences – the nourishing and productive influences of Quranic teachings.*

*The Constitution of America is influenced by Quranic teachings. Even the capitalist concept of business is influenced by Quranic teachings. The idea of human dignity that the Constitution expresses is more in accord with the concept of man in the Quran than it is with the concept of man in the Bible. And many wonder why the Chief Imam [W. D. Mohammed] now wants to save America. I want to save America because I see two lives in America. The lifeblood of truth and the lifeblood of lies. And I think that all we have to do is just separate ourselves from that lifeblood of lies and we will have a beautiful America, indeed.*

*Stop listening to tales about Arabs as slave traders. Wake up. The day of your great victory is here. Don't sleep. Do you think that an intelligent man – even if he knew for certain that some Arabs were in the slave trade business – would separate himself from the great past, from his great history and dignity in Al-Islam, simply because some Arabs had a part in the slave trade? No intelligent man would do that kind of foolish thing. Did anybody ever try to make you believe that a man, simply because he accepts Al-Islam, becomes pure and spotless, safe from doing any wrong? No. Allah says in the Quran that the righteous people are not to be identified by skin or by their religious labels.*

*Allah says, in the Quran, that righteousness isn't turning your face East or West. Righteousness is in being God-fearing, in obedience to God. Righteousness is in carrying out the wishes of God. Righteousness is in believing in God, His books, His prophets, His angels, His promises to His people or to the faithful – that righteous-*

ness is in kind, charitable treatment of the next of kin, to the near relative. And also to the widows, to the orphans, and to the person in the road who has no place to stay tonight. All of that comes from the definition of righteousness in the Quran.

It didn't say righteousness is the Muslim. The Muslim should be righteous if he is in accord with his Muslim nature and with the guidance given. But if he wants to rebel, he is free. God says, in the Quran, that if He had wanted to make people one community, He could have done so. He is the God, the Creator, and has power over everything. If He wanted to, He could make us all one in the same community. We all would be making Salat (Prayer) and facing the Ka'bah and we all would be practising universal brotherhood. We would have no racism. We would have the true Al-Islamic concept. God said, if He wanted to bring it about, He could have done so.

And again God says in the Quran that I have made you tribes and families so that you would recognize each other and not despise each other. The Quran plainly tells us that the superiority or righteousness, or piety is not to be looked for under skin color or under a religious label. It's a content that God makes. It should be the Muslim conscience. But sometimes Muslims are not in agreement with their conscience.

So, if history shows me that an Arab or some Arabs or hundreds of thousands of Arabs were involved in the slave traffic, that would not change my faith. That would not make me walk any slower toward my Arab brother who is a Muslim. I will keep the same love and appreciation for my Muslim Arab brother. I will keep my same devotion to Allah. I will keep my eyes and my whole self turned *toward the Ka'bah at Mecca – I don't care what the Arabs did or what they do.*

*No Arab could ever do those things and come out with the Holy Quran in his arms. But also question those who told you that the Arabs did those things. Question their history and see the evil things that they did with the Bible in their arms. I'm not trying to say that the Christian is bad, but I'm saying you shouldn't throw stones if you live in glass houses. And I've just pulled out a little bit of the trash that's under your rug.*

Evident in this speech, as in all the writings of Imam W. D. Mohammed, is engagement with the Qur'an as A Book of Signs that cuts across racial, linguistic and cultural divides. Invoking the Noble Qur'an without need to quote chapter and verse is part of his strategy to naturalize its message. He folds it into the texture of everyday life. He insinuates it into the vocabulary of Muslims and non-Muslims.

Elsewhere he is very specific about what the meaning of the Qur'an is, or should be, for Muslims. He offers a novel interpretation of the Opening Chapter. While the initial verse has been variously rendered as:

Praise to God, the Lord of all Creation

or

Praise is due to God, Lord of the Universe

or

> Praise be to God, Lord of the Worlds,

Imam W. D. Mohammed ponders the deeper meaning of the word 'worlds'. He wonders why the root word for 'world' in Arabic is also the same root for 'knowledge'. He ingeniously chooses to combine the two, offering a unique rendition of the inaugural command of the Opening Chapter of the Qur'an:

> *Praise be to Allah, Lord of all Systems of Knowledge.*

'Worlds' are no longer spheres of outer space or the realms of life beyond death. Instead, 'worlds' become 'systems of knowledge'. The stress is not just on knowledge, but *systems* of knowledge, and redoubled is the accent on *all* systems of knowledge: no matter what their origin or who claims them or who uses them, all derive from God. Great wisdom, whether from Caucasian writers of the US Constitution or from Arab scientists of the Caliphal era, has a Divine source.

Did not these same groups sometimes function as antagonists to African Americans? Yes, but the achievements of Caucasians and Arabs are no less God-derived. Their wisdom belongs to Allah, since *all* systems of knowledge belong to Him. In effect, Imam W. D. Mohammed is warning African American Muslims to avoid rejecting everything about whites or Arabs just because the latter have hurt African Americans. His listeners can, and should, claim the knowledge that whites and Arabs have produced. Why? Because ultimately that knowledge and its application belong to God; they are vehicles to edify, not stratify, his servants.

The obligation for African American Muslims is clear and broad. When they praise Allah as Lord of *all* systems of knowledge, they make knowledge the core Muslim value. All systems of knowledge include etiquette, or personal behaviour. They include global history, from the rise of Islam to modern world systems. They also include science. Religious knowledge and scientific inquiry become parts of a single package. Both are integral to Islam, since the One who is 'Lord of all Systems of Knowledge' is omniscient as well as omnipotent. Divine omniscience extends from the Day of Creation to the Day of Judgement. Just as there is nothing that God did not know before the first atom was formed, so the revelation of the Qur'an anticipates all knowledge that came after the time of the Prophet. That includes modern science. The Qur'an is the Book of Science as well as A Book of Signs. Sayyid Ahmad Khan and Muhammad Iqbal would agree.

'Lord of all systems of knowledge' is more than an apologetic response to scientific prestige. In practice, the followers of Imam W. D. Mohammed make 'Lord of all systems of knowledge' a pedagogical tool, from junior school to university. Its purpose is to encourage young Muslims to recognize that the Meta-Book is also the Book of Nature, and part of their own history.

'When Jibril [Gabriel] told Muhammad, "Read",' explains a teacher in one of The Mosque Cares Sunday schools, 'he didn't have a book to read, so what did he read? What was the angel telling him to read? Read Allah's creation! Read the sunrise, read the world! Jibril is not talking about a physical book; he's talking about the creation. When we start kids in school, they don't know how to read, so we start them off with picture books. There were slaves that couldn't read, but they could read the North Star, to keep the star in front of them as they walked to freedom!'

And so both the natural world and everyday life are to be understood by observation and by empathy in all times and in all places. Even slaves, observing the cycle of sunrise and sunset, could read them as Signs for creation and liberation. Like the Prophet Muhammad, African American slaves could not read books, yet illiteracy was no more a handicap for them than for him: the key goal was, and still is, to read the Signs and submit to their message.

'Submit!' *is* the message of the heavens, of the Qur'an, and of Islam. The very word 'al-Islam' becomes the leitmotif for the ideal world-view of the African American Muslim. In the words of this same Sunday school teacher, 'When Allah says, "Submit", you've got to submit *everything*. You have to become a *scientist* when you become a Muslim. You have to have a *whole curriculum*. Give up your Afrocentric way of thinking, give up your whole way of life, and *submit*.'

The challenges are double: to create a new community, one must be liberated from one's instinctive identity and merged into another, networked identity, but at the same time, society as a whole has to accept the presence of an indigenous Islam. Muslim holidays have to become part of the seasonal calendar, with Eid festivals celebrated next to Christmas and Hanukkah, and mosques have to be as natural and as welcome in the American landscape as churches and synagogues. It will not happen soon. Imam W. D. Mohammed and the Muslim American Community face a long journey. Even as they remould their own community to move beyond the wall of Afrocentrism, so they must educate the larger community to free itself from the stain of white racism. Their sheet anchor in this project is A Book of Signs, that crosses every barrier of time and place, culture and race. As those who submit to the One who is 'Lord of all systems of knowledge', they can dare to envisage a future where inclusive rather than exclusive virtues prevail, beginning in the USA.

# CHAPTER 14

# Osama bin Laden: Qur'an as Mandate for Jihad

1996 CE

Osama bin Laden embraces terror. A Saudi expatriate with Yemeni ties, he is an Afghan cave-dwelling terrorist who has killed thousands of people in the name of religion. He has also inspired tens of thousands of others to follow his path of hateful violence and wilful destruction. Yet he claims to be a Muslim and finds justification for his words and his deeds in A Book of Signs. For him the Qur'an is a book with only one Sign: kill the infidel in the name of Allah, pursue jihad as defensive holy war, no matter the cost and the carnage.

Over four years after the coordinated attacks on the United States that took almost 3,000 lives and launched the war on terror at home and abroad, Osama bin Laden remains at large. Physically elusive, he also escapes easy psychological analysis. The key to understanding him is to grasp the disconnection he perceives between his secondary homeland, Saudi Arabia, and his spiritual benchmark, the Qur'an. Bin Laden believes that the former has betrayed the latter, and that the infidel flourishes in the birthplace of Islam. The alleged protectors of Islam, the Saudi ruling elites, have, in fact, become its worst enemies.

The manifesto of his double war – against native infidels and their foreign allies, equally infidels – dates back to 1996. It was in his 1996 declaration of war that he made an Islamic appeal to fight the 'Muslim' infidel. The Saudi rulers, he stated, had become Muslim infidels because they had welcomed other infidels, the 'Zionist-Crusaders', into the Land of the Two Holy Places (that is, Saudi Arabia in general but in particular the area of Hijaz, where both Mecca and Medina are located).

The basis for Osama bin Laden's Islamic opposition to Saudi rulers is supported by Qur'anic quotations. They dominate the structure, the tone and the argument of his 1996 declaration of war. He begins by praising God, and asking for both His help and His pardon. He also repeats the declaration of faith: 'There is no god but God; Muhammad is God's messenger.' He echoes Chapter 39:23, and also Chapter 39:36–7, when he asserts: 'Whoever has been guided by God will not be misled, and whoever has been misled will not be guided.' The body of the declaration draws its force from direct citation of the three following passages, which are also injunctions addressed to believing Muslims:

> O believers, be conscious of your duty to God
> with the proper care due Him,
> and do not die
> without having first surrendered to God. (3:102)

> O people, be careful of your duty to your Lord,
> Who created you from a single being
> and created its mate of the same kind
> and spread from these two, many men and women;
> and be careful of your duty to God,
> by whom you demand from one another your rights,
> and be attentive to the ties of kinship.
> Surely God is watching over you. (4:1)
>
> O believers!
> be careful of your duty to God
> and speak the right word;
> He will make your actions sound
> and forgive you your faults;
> and who ever obeys God and his Apostle
> will indeed achieve a mighty success. (33:70–71)

None of these injunctions would seem exceptional. They refer to 'duty to God'. They accent that duty in different circumstances – as creature, as family relative and as social being; the duty is not otherwise specified. Yet in commentaries with which bin Laden was familiar, the duty to God was very specific: proper duty to God was equated with *jihad*, or defensive war against those who attack Islam. For militant Muslims, this set of verses must be read in conjunction with another Qur'anic command:

> Strive in God's cause [with the proper care that] you ought to
> strive. (64:16)

What links this verse to those previously cited is the notion of 'proper care' or 'right' (*haqq*).

And to give this injunction moral authority, bin Laden then adds another verse from the Qur'an, linked to the prophet Shu'aib:

> He said, 'My people,
> have you seen whether I am following
> clarification from my Lord
> who has provided me
> a good provision
> from the Divine source itself?
> I do not wish to violate
> what I forbid to you.
> I only wish for reform,
> to the degree that I am able;
> and I can only succeed through God,
> in whom I repose my trust,
> and to whom I turn.' (11:88)

The prophet Shu'aib was exhorting his people to oppose false gods and to seek redress for social injustice. Though he was a wealthy man, he earned his wealth by acceptable means, and since he was not doing something that he forbade others to do, he was urging his fellow citizens to reform their lives, reform them 'insofar as (one) is able', in this world through social justice and in the next world through acts of devotion.

Bin Laden projects himself as a latterday Shu'aib, claiming

his own wealth as legitimate but also yearning for the social justice that faith demanded as the necessary expression of his privilege. The word for 'reform' is itself prized in modern Muslim movements. Though it occurs but eight times in the Qur'an, only here is it directly connected to a prophet.

A further Qur'anic reference expands the collective appeal of bin Laden's message:

> You are the best of the nations
> raised up for the benefit of men:
> you enjoin what is right and forbid the wrong,
> and you believe in Allah. (3:110)

He then reinforces this partial verse with a Tradition echoing the life of the Prophet Muhammad. 'God 's blessing and salutations on His slave and messenger who said: "The people are close to an all-encompassing punishment from God if they see the oppressor and fail to restrain him."'

As in earlier scriptural citations, it would be hard to see the militant edge of this cluster unless one recognized that bin Laden's commentary refers the reader/listener back to the beginning of Chapter 3 where there is also a reference to the criterion for differentiating truth and falsehood:

> As for those who repudiate the Signs of God
> There is a severe torment for them;
> And God is Almighty, Able to revenge. (3:4)

Not everyone, reasons bin Laden, has the same capacity to enjoin right and forbid wrong. It is incumbent, above all, on rulers to enjoin right, or command good, and also to recognize the Signs of God. The Saudi rulers, implies bin Laden, have not lived up to the scriptural mandate; they have thus forfeited their right to rule.

Following this catena of scriptural references, bin Laden condemns the Saudi leadership outright because they depend on American 'Crusaders'. Bin Laden reasons that the twentieth-century American political and military leadership share the same aggressive hatred towards Islam as the twelfth-century Frankish conquerors of Jerusalem. Without a trace of hyperbole, he asserts, in this same declaration of war, that 'the latest and the greatest of the aggressions incurred by the Muslims since the death of the Prophet – may God's blessing and peace be upon him – is the occupation of the land of the two Holy Places – the foundation of the house of Islam, the place of the revelation, the source of the message and the place of the noble Ka'bah, the Qiblah of all Muslims – by the armies of the American Crusaders and their allies.'

Later he justifies his own labour as one that liberates not just the occupied land of the two Holy Places but also Jerusalem. 'Today we work from the Hindu Kush mountains to lift the iniquity that had been imposed on the Ummah by the Zionist-Crusader alliance, particularly after they have occupied the blessed land around Jerusalem, route of the journey of the Prophet – may God's blessing and peace be upon him – and the land of the two Holy Places. We ask God to bestow us victory on us, He is our Patron and He is the Most Capable.'

Here the 'route of the journey of the Prophet' is an unmistakable allusion to the Night Journey of the Prophet:

Glory be to Him Who took His servant by night
From the sacred mosque to the farthest mosque,
Whose precincts We blessed,
In order that We might show him some of Our Signs. (17.1)

Bin Laden moves beyond identifying himself with the prophet Shu'aib and not only criticizes the 'illegitimate' Saudi rulers for inviting the Crusaders to the two Holy Places, but also invokes the memory of Saladin, the valiant holy warrior. What he did in the twelfth century bin Laden proposes to do in the twenty-first century: combat the Crusaders in the first Holy Land of Muslims – Jerusalem.

Throughout his declaration bin Laden conflates the two objectives of freeing the two Holy Places and reclaiming the original Holy Land, Jerusalem. 'To push the enemy – the greatest *kufr* (unbelief) – out of the country is a prime duty,' he proclaims. 'No other duty after Belief is more important than the duty of *jihad*. Utmost effort should be made to prepare and instigate the *ummah* (the Muslim community) against the enemy, the American-Israeli alliance occupying the country of the two Holy Places and the route of the Apostle – may God's blessing and peace be upon him – to the Furthest Mosque.'

The focus on *jihad* is paramount. If there is more than one duty to be carried out, then the most important one should receive priority. Bin Laden emphasizes that after belief (*iman*) there is no more important duty than pushing the American enemy out of the Holy Land. For the people of knowledge, said a medieval Muslim scholar, 'to fight in defence of religion and belief is a collective duty; there is no other duty after belief than fighting the enemy who is corrupting the life and the religion. There is no precondition for this duty, and the enemy should be fought with one's best abilities.'

The scholar quoted here is Ibn Taymiyyah. He fought against the Mongols in the thirteenth century. Since the Mongols were nominal Muslims, bin Laden is comparing the present-day status of those Arab Muslims living under Saudi rule to the earlier condition of Iraqis and other Muslims living under Mongol rule. Not only is *jihad* the necessary second pillar after faith, but *jihad* must be conducted against 'nominal' Muslims in the name of a higher principle of social justice and restoration of dignity. The declaration of *jihad* against Muslims as well as non-Muslims is a minority view, yet it does have a precedent in the history of Qur'an interpretation. Bin Laden strides forth as the modern Saladin emboldened by the Qur'an commentary of Ibn Taymiyyah.

But bin Laden draws on resources other than the Qur'an; he also invokes many anecdotes and lessons from the reports or traditions of the Prophet, as well as poetry, to justify his case against both the Saudis and their Zionist-Crusader allies, i.e. Israel and the United States. Yet his embrace of a minority exegetical tradition of the Qur'an provides the backbone of his appeal, which does two things simultaneously. First, he selects only those Qur'anic verses that fit his message, and then cites them exclusively for his own purposes. He ignores both their original context and also the variety of historical differences among committed Muslims about how to apply their dicta. Second, he collapses the broad spectrum of Qur'anic teaching into a double requirement: first to believe and then to fight. There may be other duties but the first two – and by implication, the only two that matter in a time of crisis – are *iman*, then *jihad*, or defensive war on behalf of the *ummah*, or Muslim community.

He follows the same interpretive strategy when he appeals to those who will be the foot soldiers in the *jihad* that he is invoking against present-day Mongol Muslims, i.e. the current Saudi rulers, and those who support them, the Zionist-Crusaders who have occupied the two Holy Places (Mecca and Medina).

Claiming that the Saudis are apostates, he also charges them with failing to uphold both the religious scholars (*'ulama*) and the righteous youth. In the third and final part of his 1996 declaration of war, he appeals directly to the righteous youth. 'I have a very important message to the youth of Islam,' he declares. '(They are) men of the brilliant future of the *ummah* of Muhammad – may God's blessings and peace be upon him. Our youth are the best descendants of the best ancestors!'

'Our youths are the best descendants of the best ancestors'

is a phrase that identifies the martyrs who volunteer for al-Qaeda as equivalent not just to the Companions of the Prophet but also to those who were exemplary in fighting for the creation and expansion of the *ummah*, or Muslim community. Bin Laden reinforces their sacred role with verses from the Qur'an that seem to enshrine this loyalty as binding. Not only will they stand up to those who protect the infidel occupiers but they will also understand that 'it is a duty now of every tribe in the Arab Peninsula to fight, *Jihad*, in the cause of Allah and to cleanse the land from those occupiers. Allah knows that their blood is permitted (to be spilled) and their wealth is a booty; their wealth is a booty to those who kill them. The most Exalted said in the Verse of the Sword (*ayat as-sayf*):

> So when the sacred months have passed away,
> then slay the idolaters wherever you find them,
> and take them captives and besiege them,
> and lie in wait for them in every ambush. (9:5a)

Our youths knew that the humiliation suffered by the Muslims as a result of the occupation of their sanctuaries cannot be opposed and removed except by *jihad*.'

While there are many other verses that could be, and are cited on behalf of *jihad*, it is the Sword Verse from Chapter 9 that becomes the shibboleth, the battle cry, echoing other verses and etching their meaning in a single mandate. Probably no verse has occasioned more reflection as to its context and applicability. Since the Chapter in which it occurs is among the last revealed to the Prophet Muhammad, militant interpreters want to make it the verse that trumps all others, mandating the battle against unbelievers as general and unending.

But the actual context begins with a crucial qualifier:

> And an announcement from God and His Messenger
> to the people on the day of the Greater Pilgrimage
> that God and His Messenger are not liable to the idolaters;
> Therefore if you repent, it will be better for you.
> And if you turn back, then know that you will not weaken
>     God,
> And announce painful punishment to those who disbelieve.
> Except those of the idolaters
> with whom you made an agreement,
> then they have not failed you in anything
> and have not supported any one against you.
> So fulfil your agreement with them to the end of their term;
> Surely God loves those who are careful in their duty. (9:3–4)

Taken together, these two verses qualify the implied all-out mandate of Chapter 9:5a, but even more extenuating is Chapter 9:5b, also omitted from Osama bin Laden's citation in the declaration of war:

> But if they repent and keep up prayer
> and give alms,

then let them go free;
for God is Most Forgiving, Most Merciful. (9:5b)

So while Chapter 9:5 is severe if it is taken out of context in the form cited by bin Laden, the full text of the Qur'an qualifies its 'clear' and 'singular' meaning. Bin Laden, however, is declaring war and urging terror. He is not interested in interpretive niceties. He defines *jihad* as second in importance only to belief. He wants to take Qur'anic passages as proof texts rather than moral directives. He wants to create a rigid polarity between Muslim youth, who alone are righteous, and enemy occupiers, who along with native collaborators become legitimate targets of attack 'by any means possible'.

Crucial and deliberate is the lack of any specificity about the means of waging *jihad*. It is assumed that because the atrocities of the aggressors are so evident and bloody, the means to oppose them must be comparable. It is all-out war, it is unending terror. There is no negotiation, no compromise, no *modus vivendi* with the infidel enemy.

What is the end result of Osama bin Laden's project? It is neither an Islamic state nor a restoration of the Caliphate. Instead it promotes nothing but endless anarchy. Osama bin Laden is mislabelled as an Islamic fundamentalist. He is more the descendant of Rasputin and the Russian anarchists of the early twentieth century than he is of Muhammad and Muslim warriors of the early seventh century. His Qur'an is not a signpost but a grave marker.

## CHAPTER 15

# AIDS Victims and Sick Women: Qur'an as Prescription for Mercy

N.D.

People get sick. Some consult doctors. Others seek alternative healers. Among Muslims who become sick, some are illiterate or semi-literate. Yet they are no less devout, nor less resourceful, because they are denied the written word. Many turn to the Qur'an for a cure.

How do devout folk who are not literate use the Qur'an? They explore a profusion of formulae linked to a single Arabic word: *ta'widh. Ta'widh* is derived from the first word in the last two chapters of the Qur'an (Chapter 113–14):

> I take refuge.

*Ta'widh* is the act of taking refuge, taking refuge with God from all the evils and illnesses in this world. *Ta'widh* is best thought of as a prescription for mercy, imploring the Lord ('the Lord of all systems of knowledge') to listen, to respond and to heal.

Many Muslims, illiterate and literate, call on Him through

*ta'widh*, above all for protection from ambient spirits or jinns. The Qur'an makes frequent reference to jinns. Jinns are spirits that inhabit the world between Heaven and Earth, between God and man. Because they are deemed to be closer to Heaven than Earth, they are called jinn, deriving their name from the word in Arabic for Heaven: *jannah*. Jinns can work good or ill but they are always at work. One cannot live without the interference of the jinn. To understand and control them is to prosper. To ignore or try to avoid them is to invite defeat, loss of health and even death.

An entire Qur'anic Chapter (Chapter 72) is dedicated to Jinn, lauding their belief in the Lord of Muhammad and humankind. There is also reference to jinn in the Chapter of Scattering Winds:

> I have not created men and jinn except to worship me.
> (51:56)

Ordinary believers, whether illiterate, semi-literate or highly literate, are not capable of approaching jinn, much less directing them. It is a power given to certain persons. They too are mentioned in the Qur'an (for instance, in Chapter 43:48–49, affirming Moses's power to heal). God never speaks to the believer except by inspiration or from behind a veil. Or else He sends a mediator (*wali*) to whom He reveals what He wishes. According to the historian Ibn Khaldun, *walis* are saints to whom God has granted knowledge and Divine wisdom. They address different levels of intervention by spirits. They aid impotence, cure sickness and promote well-being, almost always through the use of *ta'widh*.

Perhaps the most graphic use of *ta'widh* by a saint comes from Indonesia. There a Sufi master has devised a protective prayer formula that can be accessed via the internet. Its intended audience is not just literate but cybersavvy. Its express purpose is to assist and relieve those who suffer from HIV/AIDS. It coordinates times of recitation with different locations around the globe. On the website http://www.all-natural.com/sufi.html, the first announcement is:

### Sufi Healing
HIV/AIDS TREATMENT
WITH THE SUFI HEALING METHOD.

The service is offered free through the Barzakh Foundation, and the site's webmaster is also a Sufi master. Muhammad Zuhri is someone who has practised the Sufi healing method for more than twenty years. He claims to have cured many people afflicted with cancer, mental illness, leukaemia, impotency and paralysis, and he does it within Islam by using the Qur'an.

The very name of this group, the Barzakh Foundation, derives from a Qur'anic verse that confronts the fear of death:

> When death finally comes to one of them,
> He cries: 'My Lord, send me back,

> That I may do right by what I neglected.
> There is no way; for that is just talk.
> And before them is a gap (barzakh)
> Until the Day they will be resurrected. (24:99–100)

'*Barzakh*' is a word that Ibn 'Arabi used repeatedly. For the Greatest Master, it became a key term connoting the passage from this physical world to the world beyond death that is spiritual, and also the space that each individual occupies after death and before the Day of Resurrection. Through their keen insight, Sufi masters like Ibn 'Arabi and Muhammad Zuhri are able to see the passage awaiting each person as they leave the material realm and before they experience the blinding light of eternity. This practice relies not only on ritual prayer, or *salat*, but also on voluntary meditation, or *zikr. Zikr* may be simply translated as 'Divine remembrance', but it is much more than isolated or random remembrance. It is a rigorous daily practice, common to all Sufi groups, but here it is also practised as a method to cure mental or physical illness. It requires repeating verses from the Qur'an or God's Beautiful Names, including the pronoun 'Hu' or 'He', under the supervision of Muhammad Zuhri, whether in person or by internet connection.

As a Sufi master, who mediates the Divine will and understands the *barzakh* awaiting each patient/petitioner, Muhammad Zuhri combines the uses of God's names and Qur'anic verses with prayer in a specific and complex method. He intercedes with the jinn through formulations that may be written on paper, bone or leather. Those things are then put in a glass of water to be taken by the patient, or buried in the ground, or carried around. The formulations can also be spoken aloud or kept silent in the heart.

Is this magic or religion, heresy or orthodoxy? Many have debated the question and they will continue to debate it, but for the person affected, it is a matter of practical religion: what works should be used, and what works depends on trust – not just in the saint but also in the agency of the Qur'an – for what is A Book of Signs to the believer if not also a book of secrets, its words portals that open to some larger, unseen, pervasive truth?

And in the case of Muhammad Zuhri and the Barzakh Foundation, *ta'widh* is a pervasive and powerful application of the Qur'an. While intended mainly for a Muslim audience, it also offers hope to all who come to this therapy with sincerity and trust, whatever their religious background. Muhammad Zuhri's pledge is 'to cure the already infected patients using every way which is acceptable by human laws and morality or religion'. For those who suffer AIDS yet exit this world on a path that parallels the Straight Path without intersecting it, i.e. they are non-Muslim, this is perhaps the most radiant light from A Book of Signs. It is a prescription for Mercy from the One Full of Compassion, Ever Compassionate, towards all humankind.

Often it is devout women who use prescriptions for mercy as prescribed to them by *walis* or saints. A Muslim woman might be concerned about an illness, either one from which she suffers, or more likely, one that has befallen a family member. She might approach a professional healer, and ask him to write certain passages from the Qur'an on the inner surface of a bowl. She will then pour water into the bowl, stir it until the writing has vanished, and then drink the blessed water on behalf of the afflicted person. The healer may also recite these words, as she consumes that water:

> And He (God) will heal the breasts of people who believe.
>     (9:14)

Or it could be this verse:

> O humankind! Good advice has come to you from your
>     Lord,
> And a remedy for what is in your breasts. (10:57)

Or a similar verse:

> And we sent down from the Qur'an what is a healing and
> A mercy for those who believe. (17:82)

From Morocco to India to Indonesia the professional healer might actually be a diviner or a saint. While he might use the Qur'an as a purifying substance, he might also use the words to mark a course of action. He might resort to the ultimate tamer of the Unseen: the Prophet Moses. Just as Moses was given the Book (Chapter 25:35) and blessed with miracles, such as the burning bush and the white hand, as Signs to confront Pharaoh (Chapter 27:7–12) so Moses's words in the Qur'an can be used to separate the wheat from the chaff, the good from the bad.

A woman client will tell the diviner/saint what she wants. Then the divine will consult a blank book where each chapter is marked with one of two coloured strings. One string has on it:

> Whoever does even one iota of good will see it. (99:7a)

The other string,

> Whoever does even one iota of evil will see it. (99:7b)

The diviner then thumbs through the book at random until his hand stops on one of the blank chapters. He looks at the colour of the string, and then indicates to the client whether the action she contemplated will result in good or evil. He either commends or discourages her, and if she submits with faith, sincerity and trust in the verdict from A Book of Signs, she will leave satisfied.

Numerology can also play a crucial role in the *ta'widh* or prescription for mercy that diviners/saints make to dispel the evil one. Every letter in the Arabic alphabet carries a value. Those numbers when added up can give you a total that symbolically represents the holy phrase. No phrase is deemed to be more important than the Opening Chapter. These seven verses, declared a Sufi practitioner, 'provide the key to acquiring riches, success and strength. They act as a medicine and a cure, dispelling sadness, depression, anguish and fear.' And the power of the Opening Chapter, for him and for others, is contained in its first words: 'In the Name of God, Full of Compassion, Ever Compassionate'. This phrase is known as the *basmalah*, and since it represents 786, those numbers can convey its power if properly used. The numbers 786 may be written on a piece of paper or voiced as a silent prayer. It may be spoken aloud as though it were a prayer or written on glass and the ink washed off, then drunk as medicine. It may be affixed to some part of the body or, in the case of a corpse, it may be buried with the deceased in the ground.

Often 786 is written at the top of a paper or material conveying the *basmalah*, but then applied to specific words that are written out in Arabic script, in order to make the prescription for mercy effective.

- – If a woman suffers from headache, she might wear around her neck a prescription for mercy that reads 'O God' in symmetrical rows of three.
- – If her baby has measles, she might have an expanded diagram of sixteen invocations that encompass the first nine numbers in Arabic.
- – If it is eye pain that causes distress, then the form of 'O God' may be written as though it were the upper and lower eyelid, and on each corner within a rectangular box

> one of the mighty intervening angels is invoked: O
> Gabriel! O Michael! O Azrael! O Israfil!.
> – For beautiful women or women at risk because of their
>   evident charm, the evil to ward off comes from the jeal-
>   ous eye of others. It is known as the evil eye, and the
>   defence against it is a Qur'anic prescription for mercy
>   that numbers the *basmalah* at top and then in even pat-
>   terns of four invokes God by his pronominal referent 'O
>   He!', 'O He!' sixteen times.
> – For women who cannot conceive, there is a still more
>   elaborate formula of the pronominal invocation. After
>   invocation of 786, 'O He' has to be written thirty-five
>   times, in five rows of seven pronouns each. Once written,
>   preferably in vegetable ink, it is then washed off and
>   drunk by the woman hoping to conceive.

Still other formulae cover a variety of distresses, from nosebleeds to labour pains, from toothache to abscesses. Huge and varied is the inventory of Qur'anic invocations in use today throughout the Muslim world. Men may be the religious functionaries dispensing them, but many, if not most, of their clients, are Muslim women. Whether literate or illiterate, privileged or poor, they place their trust in the Noble Qur'an as the medical mediation for whatever afflicts them or those closest to them. A prescription for mercy from the Fount of Mercy, the Giver of Life, is deemed to be the best cure, both for this world and for the next.

# EPILOGUE

If it is impossible to imagine Islam without the Qur'an, it is also impossible to exhaust the multiple meanings of A Book of Signs for both Muslims and non-Muslims. The Qur'an itself refers to the levels within levels of its self-expression:

> Say, even if the ocean were ink
>> For (writing) the words of my Lord,
>> The ocean would be exhausted
>> Before the words of my Lord were exhausted,
>> Even if We were to add another ocean to it. (18:109)

The receding horizons of truth that encompass 'the words of my Lord' daunt any human interpreter, yet they make it possible to gain some perspective on the debates about the Qur'an that have taken place over time.

The first concerns the authenticity of Muhammad as a prophet. In his own lifetime the sceptics – whether genteel doubters like Abu Talib, or outright opponents like Abu Jahl – were not convinced that he was other than a merchant from the Quraysh with grandiose ideas. Yet the events of his life, especially the forging of a new, resilient community in Medina, underscored both the man and his message. One could continue to doubt Muhammad as God's messenger, yet the message of guidance, hope and healing within the revelations given to him reinforced his authority as an exemplar, even as the reports about him reinforced the vitality of the Qur'anic text. The Book and the Prophet became a double authority for all devout Muslims, even when they differed about the exact application of both to the *ummah* or Muslim community.

Was Muhammad also the seal of all prophecy, and therefore the Final Prophet? The question continues to be debated. One branch of Sunni Islam, the Ahmadiyya, staked their own existence on the claim that Muhammad was the last legal Prophet, while their own founding figure was the last 'spiritual' Prophet. Others, such as the Alevis of modern-day Turkey and Syria, have made of 'Ali a figure superior to Muhammad, and so branched off from the mainstream outlook of most Muslims. Yet neither the Ahmadis nor the Alevis undercut the distinctive role of Muhammad: he was a divinely inspired Prophet, and he was the Last Prophet in the Abrahamic roll call that began with Adam and ended with him.

The second issue concerns not the Prophet but the text of the Qur'an itself. Is the normative version – the one finalized since the time of 'Uthman, the third Caliph or successor to Muhammad – still valid today, over 1,300 years later? Again, one can find instances of a challenge to the received text.

Many Shi'ites believe that 'Ali possessed an independent text, one that also made explicit reference to him, which has since been repressed. Euro-American scholars have also suggested that there were other copies of the 'Uthmanic text that have not been destroyed, and that they contain 'significant' variants from that text. In neither case, however, does the divergence sustain an argument for invalidating the received text. Just as Muhammad is the Prophet of Islam, so the Qur'an, as it now exists, is the cornerstone of Islamic belief, ritual and everyday practice.

Recent headline events have tried to undercut both the status of Muhammad and the validity of the Qur'an. In 1989 the Rushdie affair captivated England, then the world. Salman Rushdie, an Asian Muslim by birth but an atheist by conviction, wrote a novel, *The Satanic Verses*, which cast doubt on the consistency of Muhammad's response to a divine impulse. Sections of the novel implied that Muhammad 'fabricated' a verse or two, then later changed his mind. Added to the novel's sensationalism was its implication that the Prophet's wives led less than honourable lives in seventh-century Arabia. Rushdie would have been ignored had the Ayatollah Khomeini not taken offence at the novel, and issued a juridical decree, or *fatwa*, condemning Rushdie as an apostate, and calling for his death. Khomeini died in 1989, within six months of issuing the *fatwa* against Rushdie, while Rushdie himself still lives, albeit with constant bodyguards.

The sensitivity to public use of the Qur'an remains. In spring 2005 a Dutch playwright was condemned to death for his denigration of certain Qur'anic verses about women, and later he was killed. Then in summer 2005 the journal *Newsweek* published a brief article about the abuse of the Qur'an by American soldiers interrogating terrorist suspects in the Guantanamo Bay prison camp set up after the American invasion of Afghanistan. All the prisoners were Muslim, all their interrogators were non-Muslim, and even though the story was later revoked by *Newsweek*, its publication created an outpouring of protest demonstrations in South Asia; scores of people were injured, and many died honouring the Qur'an and demanding retribution against those who had defiled it.

There will be more headline stories about the Qur'an. Though they will likely concern its abuse rather than its use, it is its use that will finally matter most in the decades and centuries ahead. Scholars will continue to debate its style and content, its medieval and modern interpretations, and also its application in law and politics as well as interfaith dialogue. Muslim intellectuals will strive to understand it within the range of their own experience and reflection, whether as traditionalists or feminists, Islamists or modernists, trained scholars or scriptural autodidacts. Each could be queried for her or his approach to the text, but what they all share needs to be restated: Muhammad was the Prophet of God, he was the last Abrahamic Prophet, and the Qur'an as now received, recited and read remains the Word of God for all time. Beyond those common assumptions they have enormous differences. The feminist Amina Wadud challenges patriarchal notions of polygamy, divorce and women's worth in her rereading of the Qur'an. The linguistic philosopher Muhammad Arkoun argues for a religious anthropology that exposes multiple and changing contexts for interpreting the Qur'an. The engineer turned exegete Muhammad Shahrour calls for a process of defamiliarization, approaching the Qur'an as if the Prophet had just died, leaving this book as a guidance for his followers.

Central to the vitality of A Book of Signs is its openness to multiple, often contested views of its meaning. Nowhere is this more evident than in the act of translation. Dr Ibrahim Abu Nab of Amman pursued what he liked to call in-context translation: 'when translation becomes not a translation but a way of seeking the Truth of God, then it becomes different every day (55:29), for it is impossible to put a limit on the limitless and to say this is the exact meaning of any word, verse or chapter'.

In approaching each word, verse or Chapter of the Qur'an, one must observe the caution, which is also the hope, of Ibrahim Abu Nab. He offered his translation of the *basmalah* only after exhausting all other possibilities. 'In the name of Allah the Compassion the Compassionate' seemed more apt to him than 'In the name of Allah the Mercy the Merciful'. On this most basic of all phrases we discussed at length questions about the Name: was it better to have Allah or God in English? Was it possible to use a noun, then an adjective in English when the two dependent qualifiers of 'God/Allah' in Arabic were both adjectives? In the end, we came out in different places. I preferred to render the Arabic phrase found at the beginning of all but one Qur'anic chapter as: 'In the name of God Full of Compassion, Ever Compassionate'. To my ear the use of two dependent qualifiers seems closer to the Qur'anic tone than using a noun and an adjective from the same verbal root, or using two adjectives with similar meaning but different verbal roots. I follow the practice of the early Qur'an commentator, al-Tabari, discussed in chapter 6 above. The first derived noun qualifying Allah, or God, is the One Full of Compassion. It defines what God is, namely, a reservoir of compassion: God is 'Full of Compassion'. And the second derived noun acknowledges that the One Full of Compassion is also marked by a consistent, unending reflex of projecting compassion to human others. The One God who is 'Full of Compassion' is at the same time 'Ever Compassionate'.

And it is the same message of compassionate compassion that persists throughout the Qur'an, including the eloquent summation of the Prophet's role in the Chapter of Prophets:

> The day We roll up the sky like a scroll
> As We created original nature, we will restore it,
> As a binding promise,
> For We are the author of creation.
>
> And we recorded in the Psalms,
> as We did in prior Scripture:
> 'My righteous servants will inherit the earth.'

There is indeed in this a message
For the servants of God.

We have not sent you (Muhammad)
Except as a compassion for all humankind. (21:104–7)


The message endures, as do its critics and its carriers. The ocean will not be exhausted; its waves will sustain generation after generation. A Book of Signs continues to challenge and to change both worlds.

# GLOSSARY OF KEY TERMS

**'Abd**   Servant, one who serves, as in 'Abdallah, servant of God.

**'Abdallah**   Servant of God, acknowledging God as Creator, Guide and Judge.

**Ahl al-bayt**   The household of the Prophet; those Muslims loyal to the Prophet's immediate family, specifically 'Ali, his wife, Fatimah, and their two sons, Hasan and Husayn; Shi'ites, defining themselves apart from, and over against, dominant Sunni Muslims.

**Ahl al-Kitab**   The people of the Book; those who acknowledge God as creator, guide and judge of humankind; Jews, Christians, and others who have a Book that was revealed by God before the final Book, the Qur'an.

**Akbar**   'Greater', one of God's traits, as in Allahu Akbar

**Allahu Akbar**   God is Greater (there is none greater than He).

**Allah**   God; the first and foremost of the ninety-nine Divine Names.

**As-salamu 'alaykum**   The Peace (*salam*) of God be upon you; the most frequent and important of Muslim greetings.

**Asma ullahi 'l-husna**   The Beautiful Names of God, totalling ninety-nine in the canonical list but up to 300 for others; the Divine Names.

**Ayah, pl. ayat**   Verse(s) from the Qur'an; a sign pointing to God.

**Barakah**   Blessing or benefit or grace, conferred by God on the believer.

**Barzakh**   A term conveying the passage from the physical world to the spiritual realm after death.

**Basmalah**   Technical name for the phrase, *bismillah ar-rahman ar-rahim*, In the Name of God, Full of Compassion, Ever Compassionate.

**Dar al-harb**   The abode of war, or the world beyond the boundaries of the recognized Muslim world.

**Dar al-Islam**   The abode of Islam, or the recognized Muslim world, which is also *dar as-salam*, or the abode of peace.

**Dar as-salam**   The abode of peace, equivalent to *dar al-Islam*.

**Din**   The last and perfect religion given to the last Prophet of God for humankind, namely Islam; any religion that addresses the Divine.

**Du'a**   An invocation or prayer addressed to God that is not part of the five daily prayers (*salat*).

**Dunya**   The material world, or (excessive) concern with material, worldly goods.

**Fatwa**   A formal legal opinion by an Islamic religious authority.

**Fiqh**   Knowledge acquired by studying the book of revelation and the book of nature; Islamic schools of jurisprudence.

**Hadith, pl. Ahadith**   Reports or traditions containing the statements made by Prophet Muhammad; eyewitness accounts of his actions as well as his endorsement and approval of other people's actions; transmitted by his Companions, they collectively define his Sunnah, or exemplary conduct.

**Hajj**   The canonical pilgrimage incumbent on Muslims once in a lifetime, to visit Mecca and its surrounding places for five days during the last month of the *hijri* calendar and to perform specific acts of worship there.

**Halal**   What is permitted by divine decree.

**Haram**   What is forbidden by divine decree.

**Hijrah**   The date of Muhammad's separation or flight from his city of birth, Mecca, and his relocation in Yathrib (later Medina); the benchmark for the Muslim lunar calendar (*hijri*) (July 622 CE).

**Hizbullah**   The Party of God.

**Ihsan**   A desired perfection to comply fully with divine commands; the state of mind of one who strives to be in full compliance with these commands.

**'Ilm**   Knowledge, but specifically knowledge of God that is collected and systematized.

**Imam**   Leader at canonical prayer; the one designated to lead the Muslim community for his generation (Shi'ites).

**Iman**   Belief in God as creator, guide and judge of humankind; belief in God and in Muhammad as His last Prophet.

**Islam**   Surrender to God; the last religion of God delivered to the last Prophet through the revelation of the Qur'an.

**Isra**   The Night Journey of the Prophet Muhammad to Jerusalem and back to Mecca.

**Jihad**   Struggle for the collective good or public welfare of the *ummah;* as armed warfare or political struggle, it is sometimes defined as 'Holy War'.

**Jinn**   Ambivalent spirits that inhabit an intermediate world between the known or material world and the unknown or spiritual world; the English counterpart is 'genie'.

**Ka'bah**   The cube-shaped building in the Mosque at Mecca that contains a black stone and is the focus of pilgrimage for Muslims.

**Kitab**   The Book; the Meta-Book of all Divine Revelation (*umm al-kitab*), but also the Qur'an as the final form of that Book and therefore the most authoritative.

**Maslahah**   The public welfare; the common good.

**Mi'raj**   The ascent of the Prophet Muhammad to heaven and to the Lote Tree of the Limit in 619 CE, after his Night Journey from Mecca to Jerusalem (the *isra*).

**Muhammad**   The Last Prophet of God, directed to deliver the Final Book (itself a portion of the Meta-Book or *umm*

*al-kitab*) in Arabic to Arabs but with a message encompassing all humankind and all eras of history.

**Mu'min**   The believer; one who professes belief in God, the
Prophets and Judgement Day; a member of the *ahl al-kitab*.

**Muslim**   The one who surrenders to God; member of the
*ummah*, or worldwide community of Muslims.


**Nabi**   A prophet, one whose prophethood consists of receiv-
ing a direct message from God Almighty directed to the
people with whom the prophet identifies, most often as a
warner of impending calamities or a reminder of duties
neglected.

**Noble Qur'an**   The name by which the Qur'an is best
known, reflecting both its message and source, since one
of the Divine Names – as also one of the traits of the
Prophet Muhammad – is 'noble'.


**Qiblah**   The orientation of Muslims for *salat*, or ritual prayer,
at first to Jerusalem, and then to Mecca.

**Qur'an**   The final revelation of God to humankind, given
to the last Prophet, Muhammad ibn 'Abdallah, as the complete message encompassing and perfecting the Books
given to earlier prophets, including Moses and Jesus; i.e
the 114 Chapters that comprise the Book known as the
Noble Qur'an and also here as A Book of Signs.


**Rahim**   The One ever Compassionate.

**Rahman**   The One Full of Compassion.

**Rasul**   A messenger, whose message comes from God Almighty in the form of a scripture to be heard, then recorded for future repetition, as a perpetual guide to correct conduct in this world, and preparation for Judgement in the next.

**Salam**   Peace, specifically, the peace conferred by God on those who accept Him, worship Him, and obey Him as creator, guide, and judge, both of humankind and of all sentient as well as non-sentient beings.

**Salat**   The daily act of worship, consisting of five prayers, addressed to God at specific times from sunrise to early evening.

**Shahadah**   The witness, or affirmation, that there is no god but God, and that Muhammad is his (last) Prophet, his (greatest) servant, his (complete) messenger; the first, necessary step to become Muslim, and be a member of the *ummah*.

**Shahid, pl. Shuhada**   Witness(es), specifically, those who witness the truth of Islam by becoming martyrs, dying while fighting for the common good (*maslahah*) of the Muslim community (*ummah*).

**Shari'ah**   The collective name for Islamic code of law; a Muslim guide to correct and good living that encompasses religious and liturgical but also ethical, juridical and daily activities.

**Shi'ites**   Those Muslims who believe that succession to Muhammad was designated by divine revelation and prophetic authority; linking themselves to the Prophet

Muhammad's immediate family (*ahl al-bayt*), they prefer 'Ali over any other Muslim leader; they oppose the Righteous Caliphs and instead obey the Imams, beginning with 'Ali and his two sons, Hasan and Husayn.

**Sunnah**   The pattern of God in ordering the Creation and function of the material world; the exemplary conduct of the Prophet Muhammad, conveyed in reports of his deeds, dicta and endorsements (Hadith); the necessary companion and complement to the Qur'an for many Muslims.

**Sunnis**   Those Muslims who believe that succession after Muhammad was to be decided by the community of believers and not by divine authority or prophetic appointment; they accept the history of the first *hijri* century and the authority it conferred on the Righteous Caliphs; they acknowledge 'Ali as the Fourth Caliph but not as the First Imam. Their successors are the Umayyad, then the 'Abbasid Caliphs.

**Surah**   A Chapter, specifically one of the 114 Chapters that together comprise the Noble Qur'an.

**Tafsir**   Commentary on the meaning of the Qur'an, mostly confined to verses with an evident and common-sense message.

**Ta'wil**   Allegorical interpretation of the Qur'an, often imparting new meaning that goes beyond common-sense commentaries and also explaining verses or letters with an ambiguous meaning.

**Ta'widh**   The invocation of God's mercy and protection

from the forces of evil, specifically the wiles or insinuations of the devil.

**'Ulama**    The custodians of *'ilm*, or knowledge, who transmit it from generation to generation as teachers and jurists within the *ummah*.

**Ummah**    The worldwide community of Muslims.

**Umm al-kitab**    The Meta-Book of all Divine Revelation, preceding the Qur'an and finalized in the Qur'an; it includes the Torah for Jews and the Injil, or Gospel, for Christians as well as other scriptures.

**Wali**    Mediator; saint to whom God has granted special knowledge and Divine wisdom.

**Zikr**    Voluntary daily meditation or 'Divine remembrance' by Sufis, requiring the repetition of verses from the Qur'an or God's Beautiful Names. Often practised to cure mental or physical illness.

# FURTHER READING

Tips for further reading also serve as a recording of debts to those who have preceded me. I have consulted all of these sources, using some more than others but in every case benefiting from the labour of others as I struggled to express the multilayered magic of the Noble Qur'an. I have listed each of the several authors and books by the vignettes that accent most directly their contribution to A Book of Signs. I have given two further general sources that expand references found in the Epilogue.

## Chapters 1 and 2
Sources on the life of Muhammad abound. The most readable and even-handed approach comes from Karen Armstrong, *Muhammad: A Biography of the Prophet* (Victor Gollancz, 1991). For those who want a traditional perspective, one is provided in contemporary English by Martin Lings, *Muhammad: His Life Based on the Earliest Sources* (Inner Traditions, 1983). Certainly the most experimental and tactile account in English comes from the travel writer Barnaby Rogerson in his lively book, *The Prophet Muhammad: A Biography* (Little, Brown, 2003).

## Chapter 3

There are two monographs in English on 'A'ishah bint Abi Bakr. The classic remains Nabia Abbott's *'A'ishah the Beloved of Mohammed* (University of Chicago Press, 1942), and more recently, Denise A. Spellberg, *Politics, Gender, and the Islamic Past: The Legacy of 'A'ishah bint Abi Bakr* (Columbia University Press, 1994). Spellberg also has a useful entry on 'A'ishah's relation to the Qur'an in Jane D. McAuliffe (ed.), *Encyclopaedia of the Qur'an* (E. J. Brill, 2001), vol. 1, pp. 55–60.

## Chapter 4

The Dome of the Rock is best situated in Jerusalem by the pivotal study of Oleg Grabar, *The Shape of the Holy: Early Islamic Jerusalem* (Princeton University Press, 1996). His detailed interpretation of Qur'anic inscriptions first appeared in Oleg Grabar, *The Formation of Islamic Art* (Yale University Press, 1993) pp. 48–67, but the importance of these inscriptions for challenging polemical notions that the Qur'an is a pious forgery has been etched in Estelle Whelan, 'Forgotten Witness: Evidence for the Early Codification of the Qur'an' in *Journal of the American Oriental Society* (1998), 118, pp. 1–14. For a quirky effort to relate the Dome of the Rock in general, and its Qur'anic inscriptions in particular, to apocalyptic expectations and also to terror, see Kanan Makiya, *The Rock: Tale of Seventh Century Jerusalem* (Pantheon, 2001), especially pp. 271–5.

## Chapter 5

Ja'far as-Sadiq looms large in the history of Shi'ite Islam, but no single monograph in English has been dedicated to the analysis of his life and legacy. A capsule summation of his exegetical importance can be found in Abdurrahman Habil, 'Traditional Esoteric Commentaries on the Quran' in S. H. Nasr (ed.), *Islamic Spirituality: Foundations* (Crossroad, 1987), pp. 24–47, and a listing of the major Qur'anic verses that refer to Imams as Signs of God, Possessors of Knowledge, the Two Seas, etc. is provided by Moojan Momen, *An Introduction to Shiite Islam* (Yale University Press, 1985), pp. 150–53.

## Chapter 6

Few scholars of the Qur'an have been as thoroughly studied as Abu Ja'far Muhammad ibn Jarir at-Tabari. In part this is because he wrote not only one of the earliest and most comprehensive commentaries on the Qur'an but also an extraordinary world history, from the time of Adam up till his own death in the early tenth century of the common era. Ehsan Yarshater has been the supervisory force for a complete English translation of *The History of at-Tabari* (State University of New York Press, 1985– ) that, it is hoped, will total 39 volumes. A similar, if lesser translation project was undertaken on at-Tabari's Qur'an commentary, but only the first of its five volumes has appeared in English due to the untimely death of the translator. See J. Cooper (trans.), *The Commentary on the Qur'an by Abu Ja'far Muhammad ibn Jarir at-Tabari* (Oxford University Press, 1987). On at-Tabari's fondness for classification and how that disposition influenced his approach to interpreting the Qur'an, consult Jane D. McAuliffe, 'Qur'anic Hermeneutics: The Views of at-Tabari and Ibn Kathir' in Andrew Rippin (ed.), *Approaches to the History of the Interpretation of the Qur'an* (Oxford University Press, 1988), pp. 46–54.

## Chapter 7

An early English-language source drawing attention to the importance of Robert of Ketton is James Kritzeck, *Peter the Venerable and Islam* (Princeton University Press, 1964). More recently, Thomas E. Burman has elaborated on Robert's role by comparing, but mostly contrasting, him with Mark of Toledo. See Thomas E. Burman, *'Tafsir* and Translation: Traditional Qur'an Exegesis and the Latin Qur'ans of Robert of Ketton and Mark of Toledo', *Speculum* (1998), 73, pp. 703–22. The impact of Robert's translation during the 600 years since its publication has been charted by Hartmut Bobzin, '"A Treasuring of Heresies": Christian Polemics Against the Koran' in Stefan Wild (ed.), *The Qur'an As Text* (E. J. Brill, 1996), pp. 156–75.

## Chapter 8

Ibn 'Arabi has been studied intensively in both Europe and the USA as well as in metropolitan centres of the Muslim world. The best translation of *Fusus al-hikam* available in English is R. W. J. Austin, *Ibn 'Arabi: The Bezels of Wisdom* (Paulist Press, 1981). *Futuhat al-makkiya* or 'Meccan Openings' has yet to be rendered into English, although many excerpts can be found in William C. Chittick, *The Sufi Path of Knowledge: Ibn al-Arabi's Metaphysics of Imagination* (SUNY Press, 1989). A full-scale, if adulatory, biography was written in French, then translated into English: Claude Addas, *Quest for the Red Sulphur: The Life of Ibn 'Arabic* (Islamic Texts Society, 1993). Some of the best critical works are by Addas's father, the French scholar Michel Chodkiewicz. Two of them have been translated into English: *An Ocean without Shore: Ibn 'Arabi, the Book, and the Law* (SUNY, 1993) and *The Seal of the Saints* (Islamic Texts Society, 1993). A lucid explanation of how Ibn 'Arabi interpreted Muhammad's Night Journey has been provided by James Morris, 'The Spiritual Ascension: Ibn 'Arabi and the Mi'raj', *Journal of the American Oriental Society* (1987) 107, pp. 629–52 (1988), 108, pp. 63–77.

### Chapter 9

Rumi has been both studied and popularized in multiple English-language sources. Several gemlike essays, including one by Annemarie Schimmel, are to be found in the second half of Peter J. Chelkowski (ed.), *The Scholar and the Saint: Studies in Commemoration of Abu'l-Rayhman al-Biruni and Jalal ad-din al-Rumi* (New York University Press, 1975). The most systematic exposition of the *Mathnawi* in English is William Chittick, *The Sufi Path of Love: The Spiritual Teachings of Rumi* (SUNY Press, 1983), while the stylistic subtleties of Rumi have been best explored by Fatemeh Keshavarz, *Reading Mystical Lyric: The Case of Jalal ad-din Rumi* (University of South

213 I FURTHER READING

Carolina Press, 1998). Coleman Bark's *Essential Rumi* (HarperSanFrancisco, 1997) is a very popular anthology of Rumi's verse, but it has many rivals, including Jonathan Star and Shahram Shiva (trans.), *A Garden Beyond Paradise: The Mystical Poetry of Rumi* (Bantam Books, 1992). The table talk of Rumi, cited in this vignette, is indebted to the English rendition by W. M. Thackston, Jr, *Signs of the Unseen: The Discourses of Jalaluddin Rumi* (Threshold Books, 1994).

## Chapter 10

The most delightful book on the Taj Mahal as a tomb garden may be Elizabeth B. Moynihan, *Paradise as a Garden in Persia and Mughal India* (George Braziller, 1979), but the academic benchmark, at least in English, has been set at the highest level by W. E. Begley and Z. A. Desai, *Taj Mahal: The Illumined Tomb* (Aga Khan Program for Islamic Architecture & University of Washington Press, 1989). The link to Ibn 'Arabi's allegorical paradigm of Paradise is detailed in Wayne E. Begley, 'The Myth of the Taj Mahal and a New Theory of Its Symbolic Meaning' in *The Art Bulletin*, March 1979, pp. 7–37.

## Chapter 11

The thought of Sayyid Ahmad Khan has been deftly summarized by Aziz Ahmad, *Islamic Modernism in India and Pakistan 1857–1964* (Oxford University Press, 1967), but also of value is Christian Troll, *Sayyid Ahmad Khan: A Reinterpretation of Muslim Theology* (Oxford University Press, 1978), and the limits of his approach to science are marked and measured by

Muzaffar Iqbal, *Islam and Science* (Ashgate Publishing House, 2002).

**Chapter 12**
Muhammad Iqbal's *The Reconstruction of Religious Thought in Islam* has been reprinted several times. The best analytical study of his engagement with images and passages from the Qur'an remains Annemarie Schimmel, *Gabriel's Wing: A Study into the Religious Ideas of Sir Muhammad Iqbal* (E. J. Brill, 1963), though it can be usefully supplemented by Iqbal Singh, *The Ardent Pilgrim: An Introduction to the Life and Work of Mohammed Iqbal* (Oxford University Press, 1997). For translations, no one can equal Khushwant Singh's rendering of *Shikwa o-Jawab-i Shikwa (Complaint and Answer): Iqbal's Dialogue with Allah* (Oxford University Press, 1981), while a marvellous offering of his other verse is to be found in Mustansir Mir, *Tulip in the Desert: A Selection of the Poetry of Muhammad Iqbal* (McGill-Queen's University Press, 2000).

**Chapter 13**
The speech on Qur'an and slavery comes from Warith Deen Muhammad, *As the Light Shineth From the East* (WDM Publishing Company, 1980). Insight into the practice of his community is provided by Gregory Starrett, 'Muslim Identities and the Great Chain of Buying' in Dale F. Eickelman and Jon W. Anderson (eds), *New Media in the Muslim World* (Indiana University Press, 1999), pp. 57–79. The best study of Imam W. D. Mohammed in the context of

American race relations is Edward E. Curtis IV, *Islam in Black America* (SUNY Press, 2002), while a comprehensive overview of often disparate studies can be found in Karen Leonard, *Muslims in the United States: The State of Research* (Russell Sage Foundation, 2003).

## Chapter 14

Publications on Osama bin Laden have become a cottage industry since 11 September 2001. Preceding that deluge in French, then published in English soon after, was Roland Jacquard, *In the Name of Osama bin Laden: Global Terrorism and the bin Laden Brotherhood* (Duke University Press, 2002). It is still of value, though it does not contain the 1996 declaration of war, provided at <http://www.library.cornell.edu/colldev/mideast/fatw2.htm>. Rosalind Gwynne offers an extended analysis in 'Al-Qa'ida and al-Qur'an: The "Tafsir" of Usamah bin Ladin', also online, at <http://www.utk.edu/~warda/bin_laden_and_quran.htm>, while Charles Kurzman has offered the fullest set of references, available at <http://www.unc.edu/~kurzman/terror.htm>. Also now available is Bruce Lawrence, ed. *Messages of the World: The Statements of Osama bin Laden* (Verso, 2005).

## Chapter 15

Much has been written about Prophetic medicine and Sufi healing. An accessible popular book is Shaykh Hakim Moinuddin Chishti, *The Book of Sufi Healing* (Inner Traditions International, 1991), which also includes two appendices on

Qur'anic Chapters and Divine Attributes often used by Sufi practitioners. Further Qur'anic material online can be found on a number of websites, but the most accessible description of online Qur'an translations remains Gary Bunt, *Virtually Islamic: Computer-mediated Communication and Cyber Islamic Environments* (University of Wales, 2000), pp. 17–28.

**Epilogue**

Beyond the many articles on specific topics in Jane D. McAuliffe (ed.), *Encyclopaedia of the Qur'an* (E. J. Brill, 2001–6), one can gauge the range of scholarly reflection in G. R. Hawting and Abdul-Kader A. Shareef (eds), *Approaches to the Qur'an* (Routledge, 1993). For superb essays on Wadud, Arkoun and Shahrour, among others, see Suha Taji-Farouki, ed., *Modern Muslim Intellectuals and the Qur'an* (Oxford University Press, 2004). For my perspective on the dilemma, and delight, of translating the *basmalah*, see Bruce B. Lawrence, 'Approximating *saj'* in English renditions of the Qur'an: A Close Reading of Surah 93 (Ad-Duha)'and the basmala in *Journal of Qur'anic Studies* VII/I (2005):78–80.

# INDEX

# INDEX OF CITATIONS

*Indexes compiled by Meg Davies*
*(Registered Indexer, Society of Indexers)*